South Sudanese Manhood and Family Crisis in the Diaspora

Akuch Kuol Anyieth

A Note from the Publisher

The publisher wishes to acknowledge and thank Dr Douglas H. Johnson for his invaluable help and support for Africa World Books and its mission of preserving and promoting African cultural and literary traditions and history. Dr Johnson and fellow historians have been instrumental in ensuring that African people remain connected to their past and their identity. Africa World Books is proud to carry on this mission.

ISBN:978-0-6450102-4-4

Design and typesetting: Africa World Books

About the Author

Akuch Kuol Anyieth is a graduate researcher completing a PhD in the discipline of Crime, Justice and Legal Studies at La Trobe University in Melbourne, Victoria, Australia. Her research interests broadly cover masculinity, domestic violence, and the law. She has a Bachelor of Legal Studies, Master of Justice and Criminology, and Master of Arts by Research. Her work weaves together South Sudanese customary laws, pre-post migration experiences of South Sudanese families and their adaptation of the western rules of law in the diaspora. She has worked within the criminal justice system, government organisations and non-government organisations for the last 10 years. Akuch's work, lived experience, and research reveals many issues that face South Sudanese families that are often not included and rarely considered within family violence studies. Akuch's unique position as a South Sudanese woman writing about South Sudanese challenges in the diaspora brings an original contribution to existing literature on family violence and South Sudanese traumatic history. The many dimensions that contribute to experiences of family crisis (violence in families) including the historical context of South Sudanese men pre-and post-migration are core discussion points in this book. *South Sudanese Manhood and Family Crisis in the Diaspora* illuminates the past, critiques the present and offers an unequalled vision for a way forward into the future.

Writing style

For the most part, I have used an informal, conversational style with factual examples drawn from my work experience, academic research, and personal encounters within the community. This writing style emphasises discussion and explanation of the issues, instead of a "cookbook" style presentation of facts. An informal style was intentionally used to make the book readable and unintimidating; it will be particularly useful for non-academic readers.

List of Contents

Introduction

Sudan was the largest country in Africa but it always had this tension between the north and the south: a tension deeply rooted in politics, culture and religion. South Sudan's ancient past is part of the greater history of the Nile Valley peoples. The Nile Valley people have been known by many names throughout history and it can depend on who is writing history at that particular time as to which names are used. The names are a reference to the appearance of the people: Ethiopian, Sudanese, Kushite and many more. The decline of the Egypto-Nubian Kingdoms of ancient history led directly to the establishment of the Sudanic Kingdoms such as Mali, Songhai, Meroe and Napata to name a few.

Geographically, South Sudan is a landlocked country in east-central Africa that shares borders with five countries to the west, south and east. To the north is Sudan. Politically, South Sudan is the world's youngest nation after gaining independence from the north in 2011 after a prolonged civil war. The multipart genesis of this war includes differences in religious beliefs and practices, tribal alliances, colonial influence and access to natural resources in post-colonial Sudan.[1] After many years of attempting to reach a peace agreement, the two (the north and the south) governments agreed to the signing of the Comprehensive Peace Agreement (CPA) in 2005. Both parties then agreed to 1) a permanent ceasefire, 2) form an interim national unity government, and 3) conduct a referendum within six years to define the future of the South Sudanese. After six years of transitioning the referendum took place and the proposal for separation from the north received the highest number of votes, which resulted in South Sudan gaining independence in 2011. Before independence, as a result of the war, hundreds of thousands of South Sudanese people were forced to migrate to nearby countries where they were settled in camps as refugees or internally displaced persons. In these refugee camps set up by the United Nations High Commissioner for Refugees (UNHCR), most families and unaccompanied children spent a prolonged period before they became eligible for humanitarian visas to western countries such as Australia, the United States of America, Canada and the United Kingdom.

We all understand the coexistence of the male and female gender and the shared yet different realities men and women experience. It is the reality of this world to have man and woman coexist. My lifelong curiosity, work history and academic studies have focused on one part of the family crisis puzzle: the perpetration of 'violence' in the family unit, with a particular interest in the function of the male gender as an active agent in the perpetration of violence within the family unit, and as such, this book will focus on South Sudanese males' experiences of gender while living in the diaspora. Women, too, have greatly suffered during the war and in the diaspora - just as much as the men, their experiences are interconnected. When reading this book, bear in mind that I am aware of and acknowledge women's suffering and struggle to maintain their feminine attributes and roles as women back home and in the diaspora. I have witnessed some South Sudanese men turn into domestic abusers and the monitoring spirits of their wives. That is not a behaviour that this book wishes to excuse but should be dealt with justly and accordingly, however, the complexity and paramount importance of women's issues nowadays deserves a separate book and will not be explored here. So, if you're a woman reading this book, read it with an open mind; read it with your father, brothers, male relatives and friends in mind. The arguments and the narratives brought forth in this book are not an attack against women or a male defence, but a reality of what South Sudanese males have experienced or are continuing to experience today, which affects family units.

Understanding the roots of our struggles as South Sudanese might help us to start paving a way to harmonious families. Fostering non-violent good men could balance our future. But to regenerate this process we must first understand a number of important things. What makes a man and what masculine attributes does he need to possess? How have these attributes been tainted by the war and now marginalised in diaspora? What can men and women do collectively to assist in the fight to bring back good masculine identities and practices? South Sudanese culture has changed significantly over the course of the centuries. The wisdom of our ancestors is no longer applicable to these modern times. We are continuing to lose our ways of doing as we continue to encounter foreign cultures that have shaken so many to the very core of our foundations. Many families in the diaspora are affected by this shift either indirectly or directly.

This image was taken during an initiation process in 2016. The boys in the image were being transitioned into men, hence the shaving of the heads and walking in groups according to their social relations.

Image taken by Awan Kuol Awan

CHAPTER ONE

Pre-colonial Manhood

Rite of passage from boys to men

South Sudan has retained its many indigenous ethnic groups with their many linguistic and cultural differences; it is worth mentioning that I am going to discuss the overarching beliefs and practices that are shared across tribal groups in South Sudan, bearing in mind that the two biggest groups are the Dinka and Nuer. Due to the unreliable records of population data in the pre-colonial period, it is disputed whether the Bari, Shilluk or Zande are the third largest. For the sake of this book, it is important to present a collective South Sudan rather than tribal groups.

In the traditional South Sudan, manhood was something celebrated above all else. It was an important aspect, second only to birth for the male gender, and involved a decent amount of preparation from the boy's family to give their male child a good rite of passage. It was a time where families could show their wealth, making sure that the transition for their boy was met with greatness and pride. It was also the last time in the boy-children's lives that they could truly be boys - not the 'boys will be boys' cliché, but time where boys were expected to be done with doing things from their boyhood.The South Sudanese believed that boys need active care and teaching to help them grow to be strong, brave, respectful men and this requires contribution from their community:'*It takes a village to raise a child*'.

Initiation processes varied from tribe to tribe but standard practice involved most boys who had reached puberty from the same clan/

tribal group who were not part of the previous set of boys aged 12 to 15. One rite of passage from boyhood to the status of gentlemen of tribe was an initiation ceremony that was performed after the boys had realised their maturity. A bull or goat, depending on the tribal group, was speared to alert the community that initiation had commenced, and this was followed by a lot of cooking by the boys' families to feed them. This would take days or months, again depending on the ethnic group and whether the boys were feeding on wild-hunted meat. In the meantime, boys attended ceremonies and retreat experiences. The elders would arrange the boys' feeding timetable for a month. This program would run for a month whereby the boys were to eat in each of their homes as a group; if the number of boys were more than the number of days in the month then two homes were to cook in a single day until the final day of the month was reached. The boys then started to walk in groups based on their friendships and family relationships.

During these rites of passage, the main principles of what made a good man were commonly: *character*, which involves one possessing *social behaviour*, *bravery*, *integrity* and *respect*. These will be elaborated upon momentarily. The boys would prepare for physical marking; the part of the body that was marked depended on the tribal group's practices and beliefs. To use an obvious example, the marking of the forehead with a sharp object was a practice done by the Dinka in Bhar El Ghazal region and Nuer, while the Dinka Bor in the Upper Nile would shave the hair (*aputh nhom*), or the Alpalrak and the Bari extracted the lower incisors. These physical markings were done on the last day of the initiation that, for these groups, would last for 30 days.

These physical markings on the boys' physical bodies without anaesthetic to numb the pain were their raw first introduction to bravery. Here the atmosphere crackled with nothing but masculine energy among the young men and the elder men who were performing these markings. Bodies were scarred, tooth or teeth canalled and blood shed. After this, the boy was declared a man and was to immediately abandon his old ways of doing things and be given due respect, and from there on the roles of the young men shifted.

In the last days of the rite of passage, the boys were labelled as men. There is something about labelling and human brains; once you give a thing a name, you have spoken life to it, given it meaning and made it real. There is something that holds you accountable to that label once the brain has registered it. With the help of the fathers, older brothers, uncles, male cousins and other men in the community, coupled with mothers and sisters, the new men were helped and guided into their newly acquired stage of life. These people around them were the support mechanism, holding the new men accountable to their newly claimed title of 'manhood'. For the young man, duties in the family, tribe and society had shifted. More was expected from the young man; in terms of behaviour, they were expected to build and maintain positive, lasting social relations and perform certain heavy duties. Let's break these down into four of the most expected and adhered to behaviours, as previously mentioned.

Social behaviour

In traditional South Sudanese culture, the upholding and practicing of good social behaviours was accepted as one of the most important features of a young man. A young man who respected himself, his family name, clan and his society was always expected to carry himself and act in a way that did not tarnish his or his family's name. Young men were expected to respect their elders whether within or outside their individual family. Elders were very much encouraged to intervene once they believed a young person had behaved in a socially irresponsible manner. Young men were expected to stand firm to prevent conflict from happening where necessary and also had be ready to freely and willingly donate some of his cattle to any member who was poor or in need for survival. This generosity would make one be respected and stand a very good chance to find a wife when his time to marry came.

Bravery

Bravery was a non-negotiable for South Sudanese young men. A young man was expected to be the successor of a father and was nurtured to continue the family legacy. He was expected to safeguard the family wealth such as the domestic animals, which were considered as the measure of one's wealth. He also ensured the security of his sisters from aggressive and ill-intentioned men. South Sudanese young men were very serious about protecting their sisters; one would kill if they believed another man to have committed an unforgiveable crime against the sister. This was how serious the protection of girls and women was in the traditional society. In his earlier years, in addition to his sisters' protection, he was expected to learn how to bring bread to the table. This was enforced through activities such as hunting, farming, fishing or cattle keeping. The young man was known as a person who could hunt for food from afar. He was expected to use his energy to raid cattle from the nearby clans in order to enhance his manhood.

Integrity

In traditional South Sudan, a man was expected to possess a strong ethical and moral principle, as this trait was highly valuable. Traditionally, integrity was the foundation for successful relationships; it promoted a culture in which individuals could depend on one another and treat each other with respect. The South Sudanese loved young men who stood for truth, this was essential across their conventional society since truth-telling would save bloodshed and hatred within or across clans. The ones who stood for truth were highly respected because it was seen as a unique and profound gift beyond all others and meant that the society would love to tie relations with him through marriage by either his sister or vice versa as this characteristic was seen to be hereditary.

Respect

Although aspects of respect are similar to those defined under *social behaviour*, the principle of respect was instilled in young South Sudanese boys to grow up with a profound understanding of the value of respecting elders, the opposite gender, their clan and other communities. Children were brought closer to the elders to learn more because there was a common understanding that children and young people learn by seeing as well as listening and doing, and were guided to do the same when their time came. In return they were respected and honoured by the members of the community.

Above all, the tribal origin of a young man dictated what role he played in their tribe or society after his initiation into manhood. His overarching duties were generally those of a soldier of the tribe. He was indoctrinated in his earlier years to know his responsibility for safeguarding their tribe from any aggression originating other nearby tribes, including the protection of the girls from men from other tribes who seek to exploit and ruin them. He made sure he used his physical strength, talent, or skill to further the legacy of the tribe; and by participating in the cultural activities, he demonstrated his commitment to the tribe's norms and cultural heritage.

Chapter Two

From Young Men to Husbands

With a whole previous chapter dedicated to the transition of boys to manhood and the beginning of a good man, we now need to know - what exactly did make one a good man then? Although the attributes that make up a good South Sudanese man could be a book on its own, we will abstract an aspect of it that is highly upheld as the basis for measuring a good South Sudanese man; marrying and raising a good family and being a good family man.

In their early years of manhood and leading up to the stage of marriage, young South Sudanese men spent much effort in becoming independent and dependable practically, by acquiring enough wealth, but also in building their emotional strength. When a young man reached the time in his life when he was ready to marry, the potential wife's family looked into many aspects of that young man and his readiness to make a good and responsible husband. It is worth mentioning here that marriage practices varied significantly depending on one's ethnicity, tribe and socioeconomic background. Nevertheless, the main purpose of marriage was to reproduce and extend clan networks. Men and clans with big families were respected and feared and not easily attacked during raids by neighbouring clans.

In ancient times, marriage was seen as the merging of two families that would broaden and strengthen communities; therefore, the approval of the couple by parents, uncles and aunties was essential. There were many factors that went into choosing a prospective wife or husband, such as the proposing young man's mode of living - meaning whether he would be able to take care of his wife and children; the family's name and reputation; and the young man's social behaviour and all other aspects of character that were expected of a young man, mentioned in the previous chapter.

Once the background checks were complete and the couple were engaged, both families made sure to be on their best behaviour and maintain their good character and relationships with everyone. This was done with due respect because if not, there was potential for the marriage to be delayed or, even worse, prevented from going forward if there was a discovery of misconduct, forbidden behaviour, believable conspiracies or suspicion of the other family's reputation that had not been already discovered in the early introductory stage. Calling off a marriage (wedding ceremony) where the young man had been given his bride by the elders was rare but could happen upon discovery of an unacceptable behaviour. After the man had been given his wife, the next steps were to either stay temporarily with his family and his new bride, or to move out of his family home. Moving out was understood to be physically, emotionally and mentally demanding for a young man hence the intensive training into manhood before marriage.

The man now had to build a home for his new family from scratch; a process that involved gathering and fixing wooden poles into holes in the ground that had been dug earlier. The poles were interlaced with a lattice of smaller branches which were then plastered with a mixture of water and mud. Male relatives could help the newlywed man in building his home but most of the work relied on the man himself. Here, women could help by making sure the men were fed and by gathering enough water for cooking, drinking and the plastering of the hut. The second building stage was the roof, which was then covered with grass collected by women in the nearby bush, to ensure that the hut was watertight. A man was required to build more than one hut for the purposes of hosting visitors and the keeping of his cattle. Some men showed their macho masculine identities here by building many huts that were bigger in size compared to those of his neighbours.

Once the man had completed the construction of his huts, he would be given some cattle and farm produce by his father to assist him to start his new family. From this time, the wife could be resettled in her newly built home where they would live together and start a fresh life with those things given to them by her in-laws. The couple had full responsibility and independence yet would still consult their parents, particularly the husband's, for assistance. Their children would sometimes visit their grandparents and return later but full control rested with the new couple, in particular with the man. Parents and relatives from both sides could visit the couple and expected warm welcomes from them. During this time, the man had all the mandates to support his family through farming, fishing, cattle rearing and hunting. He was the head of the family and everything was to be done under his authority; the wife was expected to comply since being briefed extensively by her parents and especially her mother. The husband took full responsibility for raising his children in the correct manner and making sure his wife was well looked after. A chubby wife equalled a good, responsible and hardworking man who could feed his family well. A lazy man was considered a disgrace by his immediate and extended family and was often a topic for gossip. Such beliefs created competitiveness and motivation among men to work hard and acquire enough wealth for their families.

These characteristics may be hegemonic in nature and created comparison between men, yet this mode of living was not about subjugation but about upholding the way of life and the traditions created by our ancestors. Men were trained to respect those above them, their ancestors, living elders, worthy men, leaders and chiefs; to love and protect those below them such as women and children; and fight those who claimed to be equal to them or against them. These were on top of the many qualities of the traditional South Sudanese highbred men. They were built up with the image of responsibility and protection from a very young age.

Fatherhood

While the point of fatherhood was to produce as many children as possible, South Sudanese men love big families with many children, the ancient understanding of fatherhood considered more seriously the man's ability to provide, guide and protect. A man had to be capable of providing a conducive and enabling environment to foster family relations and for his children to find expression, while also providing food, shelter, security, ancestral guidance and mentorship. Men had to protect their families from physical and emotional hazards and from any kind of intrusion coming from either within or outside their local village and community.

To be a father was not only based on gender or the longevity of men's lives but by their ability and performativity, by their personal and interpersonal character and through whom their children became. A man with good masculine characteristics made sure that the same character was instilled and reflected in his children's behaviour, especially his male children. The vast majority of South Sudanese families lived in small farming villages of a dozen or so families. In these families almost every household had a father, uncles and male cousins with the exception of those taken too early by death. Even then, the uncles and the male cousins played an important role in the lives of pre-manhood boys. It was rare to find a family without a man present because a family made of father, mother and children was the basic social unit among commoners. Some families within a village were often related to one another; these family groups could trace their descent from a common ancestor and would form clans. These clans were of great importance as the different families within a clan felt dutybound to support one another, especially in the upbringing of their young men.

Image taken by Awan Kuol Awan

Chapter Three

Post-colonial manhood and the war

Among other barbaric acts, the dehumanising practices and abuse of the South Sudanese people's human rights by colonisers and the north Sudanese is the root cause of the South Sudanese's enduring battle for freedom. Various northern regimes achieved a decimation of the population of South Sudan through the perpetration of war and large-scale massacres of innocent people. Massacres, indiscriminate bombings and raids on highly populated areas led to the massive displacement of people from their homes. Many of the southern Sudanese living in the north at the time were forced to live under severe subhuman conditions in the outskirts of Khartoum and other major northern cities.

The denial of basic human needs, such as food, was used as a weapon by the northern regime to assist and accelerate the conversion of northerners to Islam. Northerners pushed this movement south through the country to assert the prominence and eventual dominance of Islam and Arabic language systems, with the end goal of wiping out indigenous languages and culture. Political executions and unjustifiable detentions were also used to control the southern people in the hope of forcing their government to succumb to new northern political beliefs.

The horrendous experiences of colonisation by the British and Egyptian forces lasted from the 1890s to 1953 and saw the South Sudanese's former society overthrown and forever altered. Exposure to the White man's systems started to move through villages, shifting and influencing life in unfamiliar ways. Just when you thought that this was enough for the Southerners, fast forward now to the 1980s, to the time of civil war: a conflict that has been declared the longest civil war on earth.

The outbreak of the second civil war in 1983, touched on in the next chapter, brought with it circumstances that permanently altered and fragmented the lives of South Sudanese men and boys. While women also played a role in fighting the war, those who went in to battle were mainly men. Most of the young and middle-aged men did not survive the war and as a result the Sudan People's Liberation Army (SPLA) started recruiting those who were left in the villages; and as the war intensified, the recruitment of the boys began. As the government of northern Sudan's forces resumed the campaign against the SPLA, the southern-based rebel group began inducting boys into the movement. Many of these children were orphaned or separated from their families due to the systematic attacks of genocide in the southern part of the country.

Some of the young boys were able to avoid capture or death because they were either away from their villages or tending cattle at cattle camps. These camps were mainly situated on grazing land near bodies of water where cattle were taken during the dry seasons to be tended to by the male child in the family. This terrain gave young boys the chance to flee and hide in dense bush to escape capture from army personnel. Some unaccompanied male minors were conscripted by the opposing rebel group to the SPLA, the northern Islamic forces and used as soldiers in the rebel army, while others were handed over at a gun point by parents to ensure their protection, often under the false impression that the child would be attending school. Male children were highly marginalised during this period and as a result, some of them began to band together in an effort to flee the country and the war. Young men and boys who were isolated and unable to independently support themselves suffered greatly from the terror.

For many who had lost their parents, mainly their fathers, and with the need to find safety from the conflict, thousands of boys from the villages of the south fled to bordering Ethiopia and Kenya for refuge. Boys travelled the long journey on foot in large groups, walking in lines of single file to stay together and give one another moral support. The journey to the nearest refugee camp could be up to thousands of miles away taking weeks, months or even years to find a peaceful destination. These young boys travelled without possessions besides the clothes on their backs and depended on the local villagers' charity for food, water and nursing of the sick. Most of the travel was through isolated regions with very little to no infrastructure to aid the boy's journey. Boys would be split into small groups with the older boys as young as ten years old as the leaders. Traditionally, boys at the age of ten had usually been trained by their fathers, older brothers and uncles to be brave and to fight back against enemy attacks. This training enabled the boys to endure the journey, staying strong as best they could.

It has been estimated that over half the boys died on this horrendous journey due to starvation, dehydration, disease, animal attacks and abduction and murder by enemy soldiers. Most of the boys became extremely malnourished, as food was scarce and could only be sourced through donations from villages along the way or from hunting and fishing. In this weakened state, the boys were also extremely vulnerable to attacks by wild animals, heat exhaustion and illness such as malaria, pneumonia and other diseases for which they had no means of prevention or cure. The journey of the Lost Boys was filled with immeasurable suffering and uncertainty as they rarely knew the direction they were headed. Experiences of hardship and sorrow have been captured in the sad songs composed by the boys and many other talented native song writers and singers of South Sudan, which describe the suffering of South Sudanese people and the boys – enough to make the one listening burst into tears. The documentaries and books such as *Seed of South Sudan* by Majok Marier, *Walk Toward the Rising Sun* by Ger Duany, documentary *Lost Boys of Sudan* by Megan Mylan and Jon Shenk, and *Songs of a War Boy* by Deng Thiak Adut among so many more give personal recounts of these journeys and experiences. These stories need to be told and read in order for those in the diaspora to know the effects of the war on the then boys, now men.

Manhood during the war

During the war the main role of men shifted into protecting three vital things: family, the country and Southerners' way of life, and the survival of individual's lives. As excessive killings by the opposing northern army diminished the SPLA's numbers, the army sought to recruit boys as child soldiers and as replacement for their fathers who were dead, missing or held captive by the enemy. The protection of women and children was a priority for the Southerners; fathers and their male children would first have to die before the enemy could reach their families. Women and children were often hidden in neighbouring refugee camps. It is estimated that thousands of boys were recruited from the displaced, although it has also been recorded that the SPLA did not force the boys into conflict or the battle field, but rather that it was a duty, an expectation of South Sudanese culture, for a male child to protect his family. This powerful cultural norm was instilled into male children from a very young age and resulted in most of them feeling obligated to join the war, even if they were not forced to.

The poor living conditions of their families, loss of their fathers, older siblings and the overall suffering of their people was a major influence in some of the boys' decision to practice mental fortitude and quickly become men so that they could join the SPLA. In addition, South Sudanese male children are competitive when it comes to things that affirm one's manhood and ability to fight and protect those below them such as siblings and vulnerable groups like mothers and the aged. The boys who survived alongside the diminishing numbers of fathers and older men, grew into men themselves over the course of the year. While most of these boys had no rite of passage ceremony to introduce them to manhood, their long journey on foot, struggle for survival and demonstrations of bravery in staying alive were enough to gain passage into manhood.

The separation of families during the war had major mental, physical, emotional and psychological effects on the population. The small number of men who remained with the displaced women and children in displacement camps had to utilise their energy to support their families to survive famine and remain safe. Where there is hunger, there is often criminal activity too; it is human nature to fight for survival during tough times. Survival can lead people to commit acts like stealing, which is forbidden in the traditional South Sudanese culture. In the displacement and refugee camps there was eternal conflict, fuelled by people's desperate state of mind and pressing environmental factors.

An environment of conflict creates a space for the escalation of violence between individuals, often motivated by opportunism for survival, impunity and revenge. This person-to-person violence had three dimensions: one was that of solo, unknown and armed men who looted opportunistically at night; these men had no objective other than looting. The second were those young, armed men from within their own community who took things by force, acting out of desperation for survival they forced weaker individuals to hand over any items that might help them survive or that they could sell in order to get their daily bread. Third were the criminal activities motivated by those suffering from mental illness. Experts say that the people of South Sudan, during the war and even after, are the most badly war-traumatised individuals ever examined with many of those traumas manifesting in mental breakdowns. These mentally ill individuals often had no families to look after them or their family did not know how to handle such a mental state without proper medical attention and treatment. In these displacement camps and temporary centres, the people's prime focus was on survival and searching for the next semi-safe place to run to, if or when the enemy attacked next. Attacks were predictable and people had to stay alert and ready to flee at any given time. Boys and men had to make sure that families could run to safer regions while they stayed to fight the attackers.

South Sudanese elders were the library of our community and society because of their wisdom gained through many life experiences. This is a missing element in our temporary society in the diaspora. Therefore, I would like to acknowledge all South Sudanese elders past, present and emerging.

Chapter Four

Manhood in Refugee Camps

From war heroes to lifeless bodies

In fleeing the war, many South Sudanese men, both with or without families, were settled in refugee camps in the neighbouring countries such as Uganda, Ethiopia, Egypt and Kenya. The United Nations High Commission for Refugees (UNHCR) defines a refugee camp and expected stay-period for individuals as, "Temporary facilities built to provide immediate protection and assistance to people who have been forced to flee due to conflict, violence or persecution. While camps are not intended to provide permanent sustainable solutions, they offer a safe haven for refugees where they receive medical treatment, food, shelter and other basic services during emergencies." Most refugees spend more than ten years in these camps before being granted humanitarian visas to safer countries. These refugee camps were forever insufficient of almost everything, including drinking water.

In these camps, people - especially men - became lifeless day by day: dreams died, health declined and food rations were reduced year after year. All means of survival were diminished due to food insecurity and people had no alternative but to continue to depend on UNHCR relief. Major diseases spread rapidly: hepatitis A, malaria, typhoid, yellow fever, Leptospirosis, Lassa fever, rabies and many more. Incidences of malnutrition in adults and children became extremely common as a result of severe famine. Many men felt hopeless because they could not do anything that would better their situation but rely on UN aid. Back home in South Sudan, cattle keeping, farming and crop cultivation by men was the quickest way of life, whereas in these camps the climate simply would not allow these same activities. Back home all food came from crops and animals raised on farms: garden vegetables, cattle, sheep and chickens. Hunting skills enabled men to source fresh meat and many other materials such as cotton and wool were collected from plants and the animals raised on the farms. Refugee and displacement camps were often set on dried land with only a handful of rainy days, making it impossible to cultivate anything and taking away the only occupation South Sudanese men knew best – farming and hunting. Those who desired to be a person of value in life could not see that anything good would come out of their life now with the sheer lack of opportunity.

Before settlement in refugee camps, many of the men had either been to war or had experienced the war in one way or another. If a man was a soldier, he was highly respected within the South Sudanese community. They were respected for their bravery, you will recall we discussed bravery as one of the prime manhood qualities in chapter one, they were respected for their service and willingness to put their life at risk in order to protect their country and people. This meant that being a soldier or serving in the military in any function was one of the manliest things a man could do. Veterans coming back from war were treated with the utmost respect, praised and sometimes feared as most veterans returning from war were often frustrated and easily angered. Those around them had to walk on eggshells for a time until he had been eased back into civilian life. This readjustment to normal life was supported by surrounding men such as neighbours, relatives and male family members who would spend time with him and narrate stories, crack jokes, recall the funny and embarrassing things their fallen soldiers had said after being shot, and relay memories of the toughest soldiers during battle. This was often a temporary comfort but not a permanent solution for those severely damaged by the trauma of war.

Veterans who lived in camps after their time in the military posed many challenges for themselves and their family members. For some, the transition from a respected general, major general or captain to UN aid dependent carried with it great challenges in readjusting to camp life. Common issues were around understanding the civilian lifestyle, adjusting to social norms that were different from those of the military, coexisting without the war culture, and re-establishing and even re-evaluating relationships with family members as many had been separated for numerous years. Many of the veterans lost their sense of authority, personal identity, purpose and self-worth as they struggled to cope with starting over with nothing other than the UN aid, which, according to the South Sudanese tradition, goes against what a South Sudanese man should be or do and against the moral codes of good manhood as it is not masculine for a man to depend on another man or the charity of others.

Wounds and grief

Many of the men who survived the battlefield and the miles long journey to the camps would also have sustained physical injuries. Some of them were physically handicapped as a result of injuries from combat, including disfigurement, amputation and physical scars. In the camps, you could see all kinds of disability from those deformed by bullets to those deformed by illnesses and infection; a wound could cause the loss of body parts if infected and left without proper medical care. For these groups of severely injured and amputated men, the primary importance of manhood was still strong at heart. One could not show signs of weakness but was to carry on with life on their own. Some would sit on the roadside waiting to crawl to the other side, or limping and walking on sticks and crutches, hanging on to life and trying to stay alive.

Just as severe as the physical injuries that led to physical disabilities, psychological disability resulting from multiple forms of trauma was another factor that men had to battle with. The emotional injuries sustained by the men during the war left them hopeless and helpless in the relentless conditions of the refugee camps. The endless conflict formed greater insight into the unending anguish that war imposed on veterans and those who witnessed it. For myself, in remembering the unsettling behaviours of veterans in the Kakuma refugee camps and what I see now in the diaspora, and since having gone to school and learned about trauma, life after military service and mental illness – it all makes sense. I now know that these behaviours were and are not only about manhood and the failure to provide and protect, but are instead also related to what Dr Brett Litz, a psychologist with Veterans Affairs in Boston, calls 'moral injury' a break of a person's ethical code that inflicts lasting behavioural, emotional and psychological damage. South Sudanese men suffered greatly in these camps with their personal moral injuries.[2]

In western countries, these soul wounds can be linked to times when a soldier commits, fails to prevent or witnesses an act that goes against the soldier's moral beliefs.[3] South Sudanese men, either as frontline soldiers on the battlegrounds, or as civilians running from warzones, have witnessed immoral killings, rapes, the abduction of young children and loss of loved ones. These are all acts that cut against any person's moral beliefs and have caused greater moral injuries to our men. Some men felt that they were unable to protect those they loved such as their wife, children, brothers and sisters from being killed during the war, while they were able to escape to safer regions and neighbouring countries and had to then sit with these moral injuries in camps; the thoughts of these experiences burdened them with guilt, shame and self-blame that distorted their self-identity as men and provoked a reflexive distrust of others. This created a profoundly intense and debilitating experience that changed how these men saw themselves and the hindering world around them.

Studies show that guilt is one the most crucial factors in distinguishing moral injury although many other symptoms may be present. This guilt can manifest in veterans having flashbacks and nightmares and experiencing anxiety, despair, social isolation and even suicidal thoughts: symptoms that were and are still very common among South Sudanese men in the camps. These mental and psychological experiences resulted in innumerable cases of post-traumatic stress disorders (PTSD), an illness that most people including those suffering from it had little to no information about.[4] As a young girl in a refugee camp, I saw many men whom my older siblings and mother would describe as "gone mad" or "crazy person", walking around in the 40-degree heat of Kakuma counting their fingers or the leaves on trees and talking to themselves. Some of them looked muted, they didn't say much to anyone but kept to themselves, while others took on excessive substance abuse.

The visible physical wounds, invisible emotional miseries, misunderstood mental illnesses, self-blame, the indefensible living conditions of the camps and the lack of a peaceful resolution in South Sudan intensified self-reproach as men second-guessed their fate, their efforts in the military and their mission in life. Without sustained stability both in camps and back home, South Sudanese men felt like complete failures and losers who were not deserving of life. A man's mind is the standard of a human being and when the mind is clouded, crowded and clueless there is almost nothing left to that human being.

Chapter Five

Manhood in the Diaspora

Will to restore one's manhood

When first world countries and the United Nations, coupled with the late South Sudan leader, Dr John Garang De Mabior, agreed to migrate some of the displaced South Sudanese in refugee camps to countries such as Australia, Canada and the United States, a window of hope was opened for the South Sudanese people living in camps; an opportunity all were fighting for. In the late 1990s to early 2000s, the United States, Canada and Australia started to open their doors to South Sudanese migrants from various camps around the world. Many of the South Sudanese jumped at the opportunity and made applications for humanitarian visas. Families, mothers and children were grateful for such an opportunity but most importantly, men once again saw hope in their long enduring lives of war.

Men held high hopes for a better life in the diaspora; a better life for their children whom they felt they were failing as fathers, being unable to provide and protect their family. Those who were willing to leave their beloved land of South Sudan ended up migrating to the diaspora with their families, and those who wanted to stay back and fight the war to set the people of South Sudan free remained, sending their wives and children into the diaspora. Divorced women, women with missing husbands and widows also had the opportunity to migrate with their children, making up the families that are currently led by single mothers in the diaspora. The men who migrated with their families or by themselves had high hopes to be able to access opportunities in the new country such as work, education, health, a better future for their children and the ability to support loved ones left behind either in camps or back home in South Sudan.The dreams for a better life free from poverty, a safe future and freedom from fear of being killed were finally coming true for many, bringing a time of excitement and delight to men's lives.

The honeymoon phase and settlement period

Many of the South Sudanese families had high hopes and great expectations upon their arrival in western countries such as Australia. The beginning of a peaceful life and the many opportunities afforded in the lucky country filled many with excitement. Not long after the honeymoon phase, the honey had begun to run out as families started to become absorbed in the numerous practical problems of settlement in a new country: finding shelter, learning English, obtaining employment and commencing further education pathways for those who wanted to pursue academic endeavours. In negotiating these practical problems, feelings of frustration, disappointment, fear, anger, embarrassment and guilt were not far behind especially for the men. In the patriarchal society of South Sudan, a man is the head of the family and is responsible for carrying out all duties that would aid the family's comfort. However, due to the new environment and language barriers, this role was taken by settlement service providers such as social workers, leaving the men feeling that their role as a provider, a protector, and a family shield was undermined, which put strain on many families.[5] This made the method of settlement service provisions very patriarchal in itself in a sense that settlement services became the head of many families other than the men. This is not to deny some of the good work of settlement services who were trying their best to welcome and settle South Sudanese migrants, however, the process and, more generally, the post-refugee encounters of authorities and environment had enormous impacts on the individual's ability to recover from their pre-arrival trauma and to rebuild their lives quickly within the settlement time frame.

The encountering of barriers and obstacles while trying to adapt to a new way of living compounded the existing psychological problems of South Sudanese families and their men. Families started experiencing anxieties about their family members who were left behind, and tried to manage their guilt and feelings of helplessness in this unfamiliar environment of Australia. Moreover, fears caused by the unfamiliarity with the new environment created further insecurities and isolated individuals from community networks, resulting in cultural isolation for many families and individuals. During the early settlement period, many men felt that they had no use in the new society as everything was being outsourced and controlled by settlement services which did not focus on empowering the individual and the community but instead focused on service delivery. This method hindered people's agency to be involved in issues and decisions concerning their lives and resulted in a give and take relationship between the newly arrived South Sudanese community and service providers. This was a time where the concept of co-design was not a priority in the settlement service sector and was often overlooked by service providers. We now see that this concept has been established and the evidence shows that this is a more impactful way for service delivery and community engagement.

As mentioned above the patriarchal culture of South Sudanese is that the man is the head of the family and is expected to provide, protect and guide the family in a manner that will not bring shame to their family lineage. Space for these practices was diminished, if not taken away completely, upon settlement. One can argue that this was not done intentionally by service providers and systems but that rather men's agency was lost as men experienced further hardship in their attempts to navigate and access services that would enable them to lead and take responsibility for the care of their families. Generally speaking, women adapt to new environments faster than men and for South Sudanese people that created a massive gap between men and women's settlement progression in their new society. Most men, especially those who were middle-aged upon arrival, experienced significant difficulties with the English language, finding paid work, managing money and encounters of racism. Racism doesn't affect South Sudanese women the way it does South Sudanese men and this is clearly shown when we look at the areas of social advancements in education, careers and representation in the criminal justice system. Having access to quality social services plays a key role in the ability of men as much as women to resettle successfully. However, all too often South Sudanese men find that adequate and effective settlement services are not as readily available for them as much as they are for women and children. Despite the number of times settlement services have been amended and redesigned to suit the needs of each new wave of migration, South Sudanese men often find themselves being socially, culturally and economically marginalised upon arrival, with little to no access to services which are supposed to facilitate their integration into the new society, not only as new and traumatised migrants but as men.

When South Sudanese men arrived, they were interested and eager to find work and better their family's livelihood but, without being able to speak English at the required level, coupled with the physical appearance of a Black, migrant man, it became difficult to find paid employment, succeed in the education system and even to navigate the social systems necessary to survive in a new country.

Many men who persisted in seeking paid employment, found that they faced numerous instances of discrimination by employers. Employers cite a lack of work experience, insufficient level of English and a perceived inability to "fit in" with the work culture. Men who have gone to industries with all the necessary qualifications required for the position have been turned down due to their accent or the recruiter's preconceived ideas about their skills and qualifications. Most of our men haven't successfully obtained work in the industries that they want or in the roles that they expect, they've been forced to work in jobs that are looked down on, such as manufacturing and other labour-intensive industries. As a result, they do not enjoy what they are doing because they feel over-qualified or are distracted by their aspirations. This lack of fulfilment and rewarding work that pays enough brings strain and frustration into their lives and again, challenges what a South Sudanese man is supposed to be or do.

In addition to all these challenges, racism, as mentioned briefly above, is another major barrier to positive settlement for South Sudanese men. Sadly, in the west, racism has at times emerged as a defining factor in the political landscape. This corresponded with the arrival migrants and refugees from the African subcontinent, particularly the South Sudanese, and emerging research continues to indicate that they can experience at times extreme forms of racism as they seek to establish themselves in the west.[6] A lack of access to adequate settlement services, difficulty with language and unfulfillment in the employment market combined with racist attitudes from the wider society has created a poor socioeconomic environment and state of mental health for our South Sudanese men living in the diaspora.

Chapter Six

High Expectations and the Downfall

For those who have never lived or been to a third-world country or visited refugee camps, let me give you some context to the different perceptions and beliefs held by those in refugee camps and third-world countries about western countries such as Australia, the United States and the United Kingdom. In the camps, western countries are believed to have everything a human being could want to live a better and peaceful life. They are believed to be welcoming, peaceful, have better and higher opportunities for education, more prosperous and inclusive economies that support those who want to improve their financial status, strong justice systems and excellent health care systems, meaning a healthier and longer life span and overall enhanced livelihoods. In the camps, countries such as Australia are placed on a pedestal with dreams of endless opportunities.

Such anecdotes and unevidenced beliefs create unrealistic expectations and high standards on what the men who have had the golden opportunity to migrate into the diaspora can achieve. These standards and expectations are embedded in the concept of South Sudanese manhood and its attributes in the traditional society and are upheld by other men and also women such as wives, sisters and female relatives. The qualities that encompass manhood such as being able to protect, guide and provide traditionally, give women the right to hold men accountable in fulfilling their masculine duties. During settlement, this recognised standard manifests as an expectation of men to quickly establish themselves financially, in education and within a strong community network. However, in most cases, early establishment for South Sudanese migrant men is hindered by many factors, some of which the women themselves are aware but do not always pay attention to or, for some, believe to be an excuse for a man to avoid fulfilling his male responsibilities.

Although some of the men brought with them skills and a preparedness to work or to seek further education, their ability to gain employment, education and pursue other areas of social and economic advancement are hindered by racism, discrimination, language barriers and a lack of networks outside their individual community. This means that most families experience financial instability, leading our women to start blaming the men that they are not working, not doing enough, and expect more from them without considering that there has been a significant shift in time, place and moral beliefs, shaped by the new environment, that often men have no power to do more in this new society. Because men face few to no opportunities on arrival, and still there are not many opportunities out there for South Sudanese men, fulfilling their family's expectations has become very challenging.

When first world countries such as Australia accepted refugees, it was supposed to be a win-win for the receiving country and for the communities that settled here. Yet for the South Sudanese it became a loss of one's worth and values around manhood and masculine identities. The right to work, to health and to education to start a productive life in their host country has not been realised; there are no jobs for them, and if they are unemployed then they find they cannot make enough money for the family. To rely on social security alone also is very challenging.

The economic situation of any country affects the working class either positively or negatively. When an economy provides benefits to the working class, especially men, they can embrace economic opportunities and use them to improve their financial position. However, when economies fail certain groups, such as South Sudanese men, and afford no opportunities to move their careers to the next level, financial stress starts to occur and compound into emotional stress. South Sudanese men begin to think of ways to support themselves and their families even though they may be devastating to the other sectors of society. Among the young men, this has presented itself in committing petty crimes. As a result of economic failure, social discrimination and racism, South Sudanese men see no valid opportunity to use their minds to come up with constructive, innovative ideas in which to take advantage in the economy. On the contrary, functioning economies encourage men to explore more economic opportunities to help enhance the quality of their life. No doubt, the economic situation of South Sudanese men in the diaspora has benumbed the financial capabilities of many in their host countries thus affecting their mental and emotional health.

Families retain their high expectations of their men: expecting them to subscribe in full to the requirements of the new culture and to the cultural norms of their individual families. This further pressurises the situation for South Sudanese men who, daily, find themselves trapped between the wall of impending civilisation and their traditional culture. This creates tension in the family unit, especially between the husband and wife. There have been many incidences where women have blamed the men for not living up to the standards of what it means to be a man. Women who have seen or heard of the opportunities in the diaspora for men to pursue better means of life, see other well-established men who have either been born or have lived in the diaspora for many years and compare then to their newly settled South Sudanese men. This is a misleading and unfair comparison because South Sudanese men are one of the most recent migrant groups in countries such as Australia, and they are continuing to suffer from many years of trauma while managing all of the factors that come with settling in a new, foreign society. There is an expectation from our women that since men are now in a country where there are endless opportunities - compared to the refugee camps where there was nothing but reliance on UN aid - they should get jobs, provide for their families, guide the children and uphold all the characteristics of a good and well-respected man.

Most women are still holding men to the same traditional standards regardless of the change in geographical location and the predicament men currently face here in the west. Back home, men didn't have to learn a new language to get employed, didn't have to convince another man to welcome and treat them as equals, didn't have to learn new cultural norms and practices, and didn't look, feel and be treated like outsiders. This context is not understood at the same level by men and women or rather some women are not accepting that these factors are hindering men to fulfil their male duties in the diaspora. Instead, men are labelled as lazy, unmotivated and failing. Men on the other hand, are not successfully communicating and articulating these challenges to their wives and families, and their pre-existing feelings of failure which stem from a deep-down brokenness and a sense of unworthiness are now manifesting in frustration and anger. We must consider the current circumstances and the environment we are now in when setting expectations to better one's life. If the current circumstances and environment are limiting men's capacity to fulfil these expectations then one must ask themself how the family can work together to manage the little they have, to better their lives and their children's future.

Women need to do this as well as the men. To set realistic expectations, we must take time to study the new environment that we are in and observe what is happening in the job market, educational institutions, business, the criminal justice system and the social context to then adjust our expectations to a level where we can achieve and help one another. For instance, if you look within the South Sudanese community here in Australia you will see that women are represented in higher numbers than men in education, office jobs and social services whereas most of the employed men have jobs in manufacturing and construction or in unsustainable casual jobs which bring further uncertainty, emotional and physical hardship.

It is not my argument that these standards need to be lowered but that they need to be adjusted so women and men can move forward in settlement at a similar pace. There needs to be an understanding and a level of acceptance that the South Sudanese community has men sitting at home without jobs not due to irresponsibility but because we are living in a society that has not prioritised a sustainable level of care for these men. These men are not being given the same access to opportunities as Caucasian or men from other cultural backgrounds. Instead of making it more difficult for them at home and within our individual communities, family members should stand by them to fight the systemic issues that are not only affecting our men but are affecting us all in one way or another.

It is not my argument that all South Sudanese men are good; some of them are not. Arguably, those who use violence to physically, mentally and emotionally hurt others are lacking the characteristics of good men. Violence is violence and it is not acceptable, yet even violence needs to be understood within the context of men's prior experiences at war, in refugee camps and in the current challenges causing frustration here in the west. The South Sudanese are people who have come a long way in readjusting in terms of their society's norms. Most men of middle-age have witnessed the harsh treatment of their fellows at the hands of the previous Sudan regimes or in refugee camps. The brutal use of force by security agents as well as other civilians who had full government support has taught them over the years to resort to violence as an expression of feelings and emotions. Following thereafter was a prolonged period of time spent in the horrendous conditions of the refugee camps which fostered many physical, mental and emotional challenges that remain untreated following settlement.

The South Sudanese people's struggle for independence over the decades has justified and normalised a level of violence as that was the only avenue through which we could make ourselves heard by those with power from the north. It became part of social norms; in homes as well as other public places, people are accustomed to using violence to express themselves simply because they have not learned otherwise. They have also suffered from illiteracy, which has resulted in a level of isolation and exclusion from mainstream society and the perspectives of others, inevitably fostering a need for violence to forge their way in life and solve problems. Criminal behaviour theories investigate three categories of factors: psychological, biological, and social.[7] Other research shows that criminality stems from either those who are born with a mental defect making them more susceptible to criminality and those who commit violent crimes due to environmental factors and their upbringing. It is important that we understand these differences in theories of understanding the origins of this violence.

The South Sudanese are facing a new battle right now at this day and age that extends beyond borders. It's not easy to be a man right now and it's even harder to be a refugee, migrant South Sudanese man in the diaspora. Because many of them have been uprooted from one place to another they find themselves constantly having to learn new ways to exert their masculinity under different societal norms and values, not only have the times changed but also the geographical location. The formula has changed, the physical location has changed, the norms have changed, even the language in which these norms are communicated has changed and this can be very challenging for any person in a new environment. Currently, families in the diaspora are no longer dying because of starvation and war but because of mental and emotional suffocation. There are so many external forces coupled with individuals' own struggles that are suffocating family units. Most families won't survive these forces if we don't look into these issues with a critical lens and from the unique perspective of their experiences, past and present.

Chapter Seven

Women's Empowerment and Feminism

During the war and in refugee camps, men and women's key concerns were around finding ways to secure safety and a better life for themselves and their family. In the traditional society of the South Sudanese, feminism was unheard of and talked about even less. The ideas and goals of feminism are much more prevalent in the diaspora, making it a new ideological learning processes for South Sudanese families upon arrival.

To give you some context with an outline of the modern feminist movement: there were four waves, with the first starting in the late nineteenth century and the fourth continuing today. Feminism's first wave was the result of a movement among White, middle-class women across the northern Hemisphere who had access to resources and education.[8] The first-wavers focused on absolute rights such as suffrage and overturning other barriers to legal gender equality; focusing almost exclusively on the issues of women who were relatively well-off. The movement did not include the racially oppressive realities of women of colour or economically disadvantaged women who had been forced out of the home and into manual labour.

Second-wave feminism began in the early 1960s and inspired women to look at the sexist struggles for power within their personal lives and within the workplace, examining issues of sexuality, family and reproductive rights. Again, the movement achieved remarkable successes relating to equal pay and the removal of discriminatory, gender-based practices yet again failed to account for the differences between women in terms of race and class, and continued to only address the needs and issues of the White, western women who started the movement.[9]

Third-wave, or postcolonial, feminism developed in response to feminism's blind focus on the experiences of women in western cultures (mostly Caucasian women) and former colonies. Postcolonial feminism sought to account for the way that racism and the long-lasting political, economic and cultural effects of colonialism had affected non-White, non-western women in the post-colonial world.[10] It pointed out the sweeping generalisations of women in mainstream feminist ideas and argued that women living in non-western countries were being misrepresented.

Postcolonial feminists also work to incorporate the ideas of Indigenous and other third-world feminist movements into mainstream western feminism. Feminists in the Third World argued that their feminist ideas should not be imported from the First World but should originate from their own internal ideologies and sociocultural factors. This feminism reflects the locality and cultural experiences of women within their own race. However, third-world feminism is sometimes criticised by mainstream feminism, which argues that postcolonial feminism weakens the wider feminist movement by dividing it. The intention was never to divide it but instead to make sure that some women's voices and experiences were not made less of a priority or misrepresented based on Eurocentric experiences and beliefs.[11]

The fourth wave, being the most recent, builds on the global discourse of women's empowerment. It champions perspectives of intersectionality to understand women's suppression. The focus here is for feminism to be conscious of oppression along with racism, classism, ageism and sexuality. Fourth-wave feminism argues that by using the term 'women', we are generalising women and only defining them by their gender and ignoring the impacts of social class, race, ethnicity or sexual preference.[12]

Nowadays we are seeing more and more female-led households, which might be seem to afford women more decision-making power. However, this is seen most commonly among the poorest bands where life-choices are the most economically constrained. This trend is also applicable to the rise of female breadwinners in South Sudanese families living in the diaspora. There is a strong correlation between female-led households and poverty levels in South Sudanese families.

Globally, there is a huge push for women's empowerment and migrant communities in the diaspora are seen as popular audiences for the ideology. South Sudanese women are invited, or should I say thrown, into this fight upon arrival in the diaspora before they have learned English, gotten accustomed to their surroundings and recognised the social norms of their new society. Feminism and the women's empowerment discourse is a complex matter, which indeed needs to be discussed widely and appropriately, but should be discussed at a level that all women can understand and engage in on a whole family level that includes the men. When we talk about empowerment and freedom, it must be in the context of good governance. We must ensure that we are guiding individuals with moral values that are not intended for family disruption and division but rather for building a stronger, respectful and more unified family unit with little room for misunderstanding of the feminist theory.

I have found on many occasions that the rush in raising women's awareness of feminism and alternative views to traditional understandings of the division of the genders, coupled with language barriers, creates confusion, leading to mis-conceptualisation and misuse of the original intention of empowerment. This is not to blame those with low levels of English nor am I saying they should be excluded from the discussions on feminism and what it means to be empowered, but the process should take all the due courses. Alexander Pope, an English philosopher, said in his *An Essay on Criticism* (1709), "A little learning is a dangerous thing; drink deep into the western spring or taste not, that a shallow knowledge intoxicates the mind but deep thinking sobers it."[13] This shallow understanding of women's empowerment for the majority of South Sudanese women has become almost a dangerous thing. This mis-conceptualisation of empowerment and women's freedom is problematic for some South Sudanese women in the diaspora, especially during their early years of settlement. It limits analysis of the various levels of barriers and disadvantages of the individual as well as reinforcing western cultural imperialism. Fair and proper education acknowledges both the academic aspects of learning and a sensitivity to the many intersecting issues and discourses affecting human lives. A process that must and should be done with purity and prudence in order for gender equality and justice to prevail.

Chapter Eight

Feminism Derailed

From my experience of working with many families in contact with the criminal justice system, South Sudanese men living in the diaspora have higher levels of substance abuse, contact with the criminal justice system and rates of suicide compared to women in the South Sudanese community. However, the majority of spousal murders are perpetrated by men against women. The question here is why is this happening; why are they subjecting themselves to substance abuse and committing criminal offences rather than doing something good with their lives and becoming men of value in society? Well, there are many answers I can offer but one should be enough: most of our men are walking pressure cookers who feel no other option other than to explode. For instance, I had a male client book me to go over his debts, which included some of his wife's that they both acquired when they were operating a family day care service business in 2016. He had heard from some community members whom I had assisted pro-bono in the past to understand their rights and the appeal processes when in debt and connect with financial counsellors. I had stopped my debt pro-bono information sessions but was still providing one-on-one assistance when I could; reading people's letters, calling companies or organisations that had sent the letters and making referrals to organisations that might help.

This man left me seven missed calls while I was at work. After I finished work, I called the number back straight away; I knew it must have been a really pressing matter for someone to leave me seven missed calls. His wife had made claims of domestic violence, taken out an intervention order against him and moved out of their family home, leaving him with a mortgage and her debt, which she claimed was actually his. With the help of a family-violence intervention worker, his wife had transferred all of the debt to his name, without him being made aware of what was happening between the service providers assisting her, the law enforcement agencies and the debt company. He was then sent letters by debt collectors.

We booked in two hours on a Saturday for a WhatsApp video call. A day or two before our meeting, he attempted to commit suicide after a murder attempt on his wife who barely survived. Regrettably, this case is not unique but a mere example of many couples assaulting and attempting to kill one another when pressures become unbearable. Frustrations from high levels of debt, loss of income and being criminalised has taken a heavy toll on men who have less, if any, support and is affecting numerous marriages in the South Sudanese community.

The western discussions of feminism and women's empowerment are not only confusing for people who have little to no grasp of the English language but rarely include these types of issues that face families especially in the lower socioeconomic migrant's communities. In addition, men are mostly not invited or involved, leaving them clueless about western feminist issues and discussions on women's perceptions of inequality, creating a gap in the understanding of safe and respectful relationships between both sexes. These discussions, most commonly offered to women, should involve the whole family: men and women, young men and young girls - to work with them, not for them. For instance, there was a forum organised by one of the family and domestic violence service providers in Melbourne, Victoria where South Sudanese men were invited. I got excited! I attended because it was almost a first to actually see South Sudanese men being invited into such discussions. Personally, I did not like the outcome of the forum because I felt they were talking at them not listening to them, telling the men, "This is what you do in Australia and this is how a family should function". This was not a discussion, it was not a forum, it was a delivery of a signed and sealed package of the Australian norms on women's empowerment to South Sudanese men, and paid little to no regard to the many other life challenges that South Sudanese families face on a daily basis. The men felt unvalued, blamed and ignored. "No one listens...no one wants to talk at all," said an older man as we walked back to our vehicles in the parking lot. What this shows is the ignorance and unwillingness of family and domestic violence service providers to include and address the South Sudanese as human beings who carry many challenges that need acknowledging, addressing and supporting, rather than jumping to blame and distrust. These issues around the disparity in who in the family is getting the most support and the quickest response from providers is not only affecting men but the whole family including the children and women themselves.

Misconceptions of feminism and women's empowerment in the South Sudanese community is hurting the family unit. There is an African proverb that says, "One tree does not make a forest". This simply means no one individual is important enough to function on their own without the support of their family, society and community. This concept is not readily embraced in the west, instead there tends to be this ambiguous push to create different levels of understanding between men and women. These ambiguities and mis-conceptualisations of what feminism means and should mean to different women, based on their individual circumstances, has fractured many South Sudanese families and is a daily contributor to the overall family crisis.

Empowerment shouldn't be about me myself and I with a mentality that everybody else comes second or, even worse, trying to break others down. Empowerment is for you as a person and gives us power to help those around us be better. Though this might not be a suitable alternative for a woman who is experiencing physical violence, it is a baseline or a starting point to understanding women's empowerment within the South Sudanese community. Empowerment is not for women to stand on men by attacking them, but to experience equal treatment and equal benefits in their families and in society in general.

We need to ask ourselves, with the global push for women's empowerment and feminism, are our families, personal lives and challenges bettering or worsening? Is the collective idea of women's freedom and equality really making us equal or is it just an idea we have been sucked into by the media and those who call themselves experts while our class, race and personal challenges remain? We need to begin with a basic understanding of human behaviour, which will enable us to look at struggling human beings such as the South Sudanese men, to be able to see their own individual challenges with compassion. Once we can understand and empathise with the behavioural struggles that they don't choose to have, their healing and restorative paths would be easier.

There is a root cause to almost every behaviour, in most cases it is the individual's family of origin. No one wakes up one day and decides to be a certain way. Every individual has been largely programmed by prenatal, perinatal and postnatal factors.[14] It takes self-awareness to rise above behaviour challenges and not everyone in the South Sudanese community has it yet. There are many people who are resigned to fate, believing that their fate is sealed. A lack of awareness is also why many people are judgemental and show no compassion to South Sudanese men, seeing them as imperfect human beings who appear toxic and hegemonic in their nature.

You have read in the previous chapters about South Sudanese men in war and their experiences of displacement in refugee camps, and how these experiences have caused many illnesses and traumas that are yet to be treated and cured if possible. However, in addition to that, psychology and human behavioural studies have proven to us over many years that what we are as human beings, and how we behave or treat one another, is largely shaped by three key factors. Prenatal, perinatal and postnatal. Prenatal factors are what happens in the womb. Examples of negative prenatal factors include substance use by the mother or emotions she experienced such as anger, fear, and grief. We can understand that such people are born already condemned to possess certain undesirable character traits.[15] Others are predisposed to behavioural struggles because their mothers regretted the pregnancy and wished death to the baby they were carrying. Perinatal factors are the circumstances around the birth process such as a prolonged labour or birth injuries, both of which were quite common among South Sudanese mothers who gave birth where medical attention was unavailable.[16] Finally, postnatal factors are what occurs within the first seven years of life which inform the child's brain development.[17] This period of life wasn't easy for the South Sudanese men either because most of the men had to spend childhood fending for their life in survival mode, if they were not serving in the army as soldiers. For example, the Lost Boys were at the peak of this bracket when they left Sudan on foot. They were denied their right to be children but rather a human being focused on survival. For us, to know one's human life experience started off in this manner should makes us not seek to blame him for his behaviour struggles. Struggling individuals need guidance to do a comprehensive history-taking in order to get to the root cause of their struggles. Many don't understand why they are the way they are; they need help to understand where they are coming from so that they can take charge of their lives, present and future. Unfortunately, most 'feminist' critics blame, belittle, condemn and even gossip about their struggling men in the South Sudanese community, only making their struggles worse.

Human beings don't simply choose to behave out of order, they are shaped by these diverse factors. If a tree breaks as a result of a storm, the roots were weak. The same case applies to human beings. A man or woman with weak roots (as from prenatal, perinatal and postnatal factors) can easily break under pressure. A man or woman with strong roots bends as a result of challenges, learns lessons and becomes stronger. Childhood baggage is almost the number one cause of adulthood mental and behavioural struggles that include depression, anxiety, self-harm and self-sabotage, substance abuse, suicide, rage, spousal abuse and murder. South Sudanese men who abuse their spouses in a rage of anger usually have baggage from childhood and adulthood trauma that becomes compounded with their current challenges living in the diaspora. They bleed on the people who didn't cut them. Bottled up emotional baggage needs to be released safely in small doses until one is set free, otherwise one day there comes a massive explosion like a volcanic eruption and you can almost guarantee casualties. Very unfortunate for the couple in my previous example.

As important as the feminism movement and theory has been, our South Sudanese women need to be emotionally accountable in their actions and decision-making and for the ideas they buy into from Eurocentric women. Understand that I am not against feminism, feminism was meant for good, but now some women have hijacked it and it has been distorted through varying levels of literacy. The ideas of and the argument for feminism are getting stronger in some groups of women whereas others with little real understanding of the true concepts have derailed its meaning and application with terrible implications. The more there is writing on feminism by people from within individual communities coupled with grassroots and properly informed discussions, the more the minority women are allowed to seek clarification; to apply logical reasoning in their relationship; to understand all the different dimensions of feminism. These types of women, for instance the South Sudanese women, are no longer in charge of their own relationships, instead their relationships are being run by those on the outside, the so-called experts. The current culture of man-bashing language and practices that the South Sudanese have stepped into in the diaspora has majorly contributed to triggering and bringing out the worst behaviour in some of our women - everything from self-entitled and narcissistic behaviour, to the excesses of the #MeToo era. Women's senseless buying into the current over-feminised, gynocentric society has deepened the silent suffering of South Sudanese men. Gender equality is being confused with gender punishment and until we understand this thoroughly, South Sudanese men's masculine identities will continue to suffocate, violent outbursts in families will continue and women themselves will remain largely affected.

South Sudanese women are some of the strongest women I have ever come across. They have endured so much during the war alongside men and in the refugee camps. They used to know how to run their own home based on their own circumstances and experience in life but now most women have laid back, leaving it to what the experts say they should do, how they should live, how they should treat the men in their life and how to live as a woman. In other words, the so-called experts are the ones running every other woman's home and life; they are the ones with the voice and because they are the ones with a voice in this feminist discourse every other woman is following them. This dogged approach is problematic and it's not catering for every woman – obviously, because there are higher rates of separated and divorced women, more unmarried women and lots of single mothers with children who lack fathers or male role model in their lives now in the South Sudanese community, than when we were living in the traditional society and refugee camps. The message has been somewhat misunderstood, misinterpreted, and misused. The real message of feminism and gender equality has gotten lost in translation, interpretation and understanding. We need re-education.

Men in general do not verbally express much when it comes to issues that are facing them, issues they are struggling with either outside home or at home. But there is another layer that is affecting South Sudanese men nowadays and that is the amount of pressure inflicted from the racism, discrimination and dictation of gender roles that some of them have become muted, completely logged out emotionally. Some of them just cannot take it anymore. Fighting battles of gender identity and roles within their home, fighting identity battles among other men and fighting for equal treatment in society is an exhausting battle. If we can't look at ourselves, re-evaluate what we are doing and what went wrong, chances are we will soon have no sane, well-functioning, capable and healthy men within our community and in the general society.

We also have a group of men who genuinely believe in equality between men and women but who are being majorly affected by the confused concepts of gender roles and equality from other members of their community. Men who can't stand men of authority or men who maltreat their children because either they grew up without a father because he was killed during the war or was always away in the army so the mother had raised them; or they grew up in a hostile environment and really hated their father or the other men that failed to make the household a peaceful place for them, mother and siblings. These are the men who recognise that they are now living in a country where they can be fully involved in raising their children without being taken away to serve in the military, and they want to be more involved in their family's life in spite of the many challenges they might be experiencing. This group of men want their wife to have and experience what their mother did not. They have adapted well to changes in gender roles and duties. They're more flexible and fluid in their relationship as to who does what in and outside the home. These men, for example, can cook and help the wife clean and look after their children; they take the children to school, the library, and recreational activities. They are the type that would attend a community event with their wife and children and sit on the side to look after the little ones while the woman enjoys herself in the company of other women. But this group don't have it easy either: their caring and homey behaviour is actually rejected, not only by other men but most of the time by women within the community.

Their wife is often talked about in a negative way either by her immediate in-laws, self-appointed community in-laws or, in this technological day and age, we also have social media in-laws. She's often told that she has subordinated her husband, that she has become the man when he should be; that she's the one wearing the pants. The man himself becomes a laughing-stock, not only among his fellow men but also the women within the community. He is often marginalised by other men and if not marginalised they will try to convince him to stop being so much of a "woman" in his home. I have come across and have talked to good men who are experiencing this gender-performative dilemma and they're often hurt more by the rejection of women against their caring behaviour, or should I say personality, than by the judgement and marginalisation from their fellow men. This is part of the reason why I say there has been misunderstanding, misinterpretation and misuse of gender equality and feminism theory within the South Sudanese community, which really needs to be corrected and straightened out. In a nutshell, among many others, the original intentions for the feminist movement were to create gender equality: equal treatment, equal gender roles, equal pay and employment opportunities and equality in social and human rights. The negative reactions towards a man who is trying to comply with these standards of equality is on the contrary to what women say they want from gender roles and equality. Again, my point here is not to blame women but simply to say that we might need to re-study our understanding of the concept of women's empowerment and feminism. Feminism is being derailed and is now heading in a direction it was not intended for. The original intention was not to break down families, marginalise and severely affect certain groups of men over others, but to create non-violent relationships, equality, peace and respect for both genders.

In the instances where there is alleged or perpetrated violence in the family, that being either between intimate partners or among other family members, the stigma on South Sudanese men and the level of violence sometimes clouds the proper due process of a course of investigation by the law enforcement agencies and service providers. This is especially common when the alleged perpetrator is a man. For instance, I interpreted once for a middle-aged man in an interview with a law enforcement agency. He had allegedly committed an assault and was asked to "briefly explain" what happened. The interviewer asked him to be brief and had added that, "We don't have all day." The man tried to explain himself through me as his interpreter and anyone who has used an interpreter before can attest to the fact that things take double the time when interpreting is involved. This can frustrate many of the law enforcement officials who are often overloaded and overwhelmed by their number of cases.

The interviewer was rushing the client and me as his interpreter. The client could sense that he was being rushed because I was starting to rush which meant I was not allowing him enough time to think and to answer the question. He tried to speak fast, I tried to interpret as quickly as possible to the interviewer, but that wasn't fast enough. The client finally burst out with, "You know what - let's just make this process as fast as he wants it. I did it, I did it because in that moment I was not a man, I was a walking-bomb and I burst, I exploded. I don't know why I burst at him but you know even if it wasn't him, it could've been anybody or anything anyway because, like I said, I was a bomb. I don't know who or what I am since I stepped foot in this country." He paused and said, "Now tell him that and let him move on to whatever the next thing is he's rushing to." I interpreted back to the interviewer who said, "Tell him in this country, people can't just explode." He closed the file, signed me off and walked me to the door.

Hundreds of questions rushed through my head as I walked towards a private space in the building so I could wait for the client to leave the building. I thought about what my client had said, a "timebomb" who was going to explode anyway. The power dynamic and the numerous layers of barriers in this setting automatically place the South Sudanese man in a vulnerable position before we can even start to look at what took place between him and the victim. The lack of interest from the officer to treat him as innocent until proven guilty was not the only appearance of injustice but also demonstrates the system's lack of interest in the causes of the crime - discovering why this man was a timebomb ready to explode. Showing interest in the man's undesirable and difficult life circumstances could have led to service referrals to organisations that might have assisted with some aspects of his challenges. Yet instead, the officer only cared about the matter at hand, the crime that had been committed, not why or what might have caused him to commit it. There is lots of talk around taking a holistic approach when providing services for some of our most traumatised migrants and refugees in the diaspora but application in practice still remains questionable.

The well-intentioned yet patriarchal approach to service provision means that men are shut out of being able to exercise their most basic masculine practices: to provide for their family. The service model risks infantilising and demasculinising men as they are left without agency to make decisions for themselves or their family's welfare. Most services are not making it easier for a man to seek help without their issues and concerns being judged or marginalised as unimportant. We should not wait until we are at a point where we are in contact with the criminal justice system to address these things just because at this point there's almost nothing to lose. Interactions with the justice system are often the first time that men have to open up about their mental health, past traumas and how they're feeling. But this comes at a crisis point, not earlier, and this is one of the biggest issues that contributes to violent outbursts. At this stage the damage has long been done; damage to themselves and to those around them. It should not be like that at all. Though there are many triggers encountered every day, holding on to these traumas until the man is triggered is a catalyst to explosion or implosion. The void, and the feeling of inadequacy among South Sudanese men in the diaspora, not only affects them mentally, physically, spiritually and emotionally but it also affects the function of the whole family and the community at large.

South Sudanese men's masculinities as emerging men in a western society are subdued and in doubt when they lack economic power and equality among other men. Economic privileges such as employment and education enable men to take care of their families as heteronormative breadwinners which, very much in South Sudanese culture, creates peace and strengthens relationships. Poverty, experiences of war trauma and refugee camps, discrimination, social inequalities and mental health in South Sudanese men can be incredibly frustrating and disempowering, as there are fewer viable opportunities to strengthen their masculinities and construct alternative masculinities without resorting to violence. While South Sudanese men are deeply invested and committed to their cultural obligations of being protectors and providers for their families, it appears most of them are suffering within a system which is failing them. This system frustrates South Sudanese men, yet the criminal justice system and their current society requires them to maintain respectful relationships, achieve social power and positioning in the gender hierarchies by adequately fulfilling varying ideals of masculinity. Acknowledging the range of conflicting forces, ambiguities, and vulnerabilities among South Sudanese men in the diaspora is an important contribution to gender critical and violence scholarship that gives a simplistic representation of the meaning of manhood and its relationship to perpetrations and victimisations of family violence. Some of these vulnerabilities as mentioned in the previous chapters include economic challenges, trauma, challenges in learning social norms and the cross-cultural communication barriers for most men. Here, I mean barriers in a sense of being able to contextualise the message, to understand the communication cues beyond words alone. This continues to remain a hindering aspect of their day-to-day communication with Anglo-Saxon westerners.

Chapter Nine

English Language Challenges for Older Men

The English language is sophisticated and difficult to learn, especially in the adult years. Children naturally learn new languages faster than adults and this has been the case with the South Sudanese of whom most migrated to the diaspora late into the adult years. The English language has many different contexts when it comes to communication, compared to many of the ethnic languages from South Sudan that we speak here in the diaspora. The meaning in the English wording of a phrase can sometimes mean different things in our native languages. This can create misunderstandings and misinterpretation of what is being said either in English or in the native language. In my liaison work between South Sudanese-Australians and Anglo-Saxon Australians I have witnessed this countless times. For example, an Anglo-Saxon Australian's way of asking a victim of domestic violence whether her partner is sexually abusive might be worded in English as, "Is your former/current husband/partner sexually abusive?" Any Anglo-Saxon Australian knows what those words mean but when we translate the phrase into one of the South Sudanese native languages, Dinka for instance, we would need a couple of sentences for the term 'sexually abusive' to make sense to the Dinka speaking person. This does not necessarily mean that the concept of sexual abuse does not exist in the South Sudanese culture, but rather that the language used to explain or report it is not a matter of using the two words to describe it. When translating or interpreting these two words into a native language of the South Sudanese, there are cultural sensitivities that need to be considered. When translating across cultures, there are cultural factors that can be very difficult to make sense of or translate.

Another common example is that when the police, or any other service provider, interview a perpetrator or a victim, they expect him or her to look at them when answering the interview questions. However, expectations of maintaining eye contact can be perceived differently. In the west, eye contact is a social cue that a person is confident and sincere in what they are saying. It is usually a sign that they are honest and are telling the truth, whereas where we come from it is viewed as sign of respect and politeness not to maintain eye contact. Avoiding eye contact in the South Sudanese context, in the South Sudanese unwritten law of communication, indicates respect rather than dishonesty and discomfort or a lack of interest. What is normal for the native language speaking person means that some explanations of such meta-messages are lost or not acknowledged because they assume that the meaning behind these actions is self-evident and logical.

What's more, the notion of cross-cultural communication encompasses a lot more than just being able to speak several languages or communicate with those who come from different countries. Cross-cultural communication also includes and accommodates communication by speakers from the same country but who are of a different class, region, gender or age. Uses of paralinguistic and prosodic features are common in South Sudanese culture and are, most likely, interpreted differently in conversation with English speaking persons. Such paralinguistic and prosodic features are things like voice pitch, tone, pacing, head nodding, hand gestures, pauses to create or maintain the conversational cohesion or show an attitude towards what is being said. A common way for South Sudanese to imply their agreement to a question asked is to use hand gestures instead of saying the word "yes". These signals, which linguistics call "contextualisation cues", are automatic in South Sudanese communication; one does not stop and think, "Now that I am using a loud voice to express myself, will that be perceived as anger by an English speaker?" If you combine such loud self-expression with a seven-foot-tall South Sudanese man, people are more likely to automatically perceive him as angry or aggressive, without thinking about what kind of impression that tone of voice, volume, pacing or pitch means in his culture. This is particularly problematic for South Sudanese who might have been suspected of criminal activities.

For example, in a police interview, a perpetrator such one of my clients who was termed "a timebomb ready to explode" may seem reserved, non-cooperative or angry due to their discomfort, which can result in them using long pauses between their responses. There are cultural differences in the length of pauses expected by speakers within and between turns. Whichever party expects fewer pauses will repeatedly and predictably be the first to interpret a pause as their turn to speak again. They may view the other person's pause as them having nothing to say, being non-cooperative or displaying a lack of engagement. This is problematic given the interrogative nature of both police interviews and court trials under the English system and makes it difficult for South Sudanese men to make sense of the western process. For our women, this pause-taking is usually interpreted as the result of the woman being deeply saddened, of deep suffering and in need of help rather than anger, whereas for South Sudanese men this is mostly perceived as being an angry and a violent man.

John Mashar: is a graudate from Macquarie University in Sydney, Australia.

Chapter Ten

Young Men in the Diaspora

As discussed in chapters one and two, a young man in the traditional South Sudanese society is expected to be the successor to his father and is nurtured to continue the family legacy. He is expected to safeguard the family wealth, for instance the domestic animals, which are considered the measure of one's wealth. He also ensures the security of his sisters from aggressive and ill-intentioned men. He is expected to learn how to bring bread to the table in his earlier years and this is enforced through activities such as hunting, farming and fishing. A male child is known as a person who should be able to hunt for food from afar. He is expected to use his energy to raid cattle from the nearby clans in order to enhance his manhood. In contemporary times, these attributes can easily be replaced by education, which can foster young men into successful careers and businesses in the diaspora. Male children are given ample chances to attend school in order to acquire skills that will optimise their employability in the job market.

Young South Sudanese men face challenges from a wide range of factors, even when they want and strive to become responsible men of value and character. When society cannot function effectively, it collapses, and this is what is happening in South Sudanese families. First, let's talk about the trend of missing father figures and male role models and how it affects the young boys. We now have an increasing number of single-mother households and with a lack of good role models and father figures, our young men are getting lost between two worlds while the older men are suffering from mental illnesses and a desperation to retain or reclaim their masculine identities and self-worth. The absence of a father either emotionally, mentally or physically affects the children: both boys and girls need fathers who are fully present and active, rather than present but muted, but for boys, it is a critical part in their formative years. South Sudanese boys are so starved for male input that they now seek it elsewhere with bad or good company. Nowadays, teenage "gangs" are made up of boys whose fathers are either absent or have gone mute and withdrawn emotionally. I cringe to use the word "gangs" for it has been exploited and constantly misused in the media and other channels, but it is the right word in this context. Whether it is the teenagers hanging around shopping centres, being chased down at night by the police after having misbehaved in clubs, or the ones throwing things and raging out on their mum and younger siblings at home - all are missing out on a common thing: good, emotionally and mentally present men to guide them into correct adult and manhood.

Binge drinking by men and boys is a community disaster right now. Huge numbers of young boys congregate in each other's houses to drink or sometimes walk around off their faces on alcohol. Alcohol consumption is against their South Sudanese culture which mandates that alcohol is for the aged, but the biggest question: is why are they seeking comfort from a bottle and from young people like themselves? In traditional South Sudanese society, the teenage years are critical; at this age, young boys should be around emotionally, mentally and physically capable and respected older men who provide guidance and train them into manhood, prepare them for initiation and take them on trips to different villages to create opportunities to meet other well-respected and capable men. Now, in the diaspora, fathers have their own battles and demons to fight and the gap between teenage boys and fathers is widening. This gap keeps widening for several reasons: fathers are emotionally, mentally or even physically absent; the role of a father has been taken up by the state where state interventions such as child protection have taken over the father's role; young men are lost between the two worlds; they are not performing as they should be in areas such as education; and finally, young men who are raised by single mothers are starved and robbed of a stable father figure. As much as a mother can try to bring up a good young man, the position of a father will always remain empty in the young person's life. There comes a point in a South Sudanese young man's life where a father figure is in need. There are certain things a young man cannot discuss or finds it awkward to discuss with his mother just as much a young woman would with her father.

As the arguably "African", or to be more specific, South Sudanese youth gang violence increased in Victoria, almost every retail store and publicly used space adopted and increased their risk management and safety systems through the employment of security guards. In the South Sudanese culture, the elders are the security system that teaches and keeps the public peace as much as at home; it's not the owner of the public space's responsibility, either government or privately-owned, to keep youth delinquency out of the space, the elders act as the moral police for the emerging younger generation. This system of operation has many benefits: such a system lifts the burden off the owner of the space; it gives the responsibility of respecting elders and employment of good public behaviour onto the young person, which means they have to learn to measure and respect themselves in public; the young person has a moral duty taught to him from the moment of birth to always respect his elders and is more likely to be inclined to listen and avert themselves from any delinquent behaviour in their presence; the young person is more likely to fear the possibilities of being reported to his parents by the witnessing elder upon their disobedient behaviour; and it gives elders value and permission to channel their wisdom of good morals, appropriate public behaviour and the importance of being a good citizen of the society into the young men and young women. These ways of safe-guiding youth public behaviours are no longer there in the diaspora simply because; the community has more young people than elders, the state and business feel more secure using their own security and also, they are perceived as violent young men for whom the only appropriate response is a punitive response.

The fathers who survived the war returned damaged and remain so - I say remain in the sense that they haven't received any kind of trauma treatment that could create a pathway to possibilities of healing. Most are tormented by PTSD and all sorts of mental illnesses yet are treated like criminals because we live in a society where a poor mental state coupled with pressing circumstances are easily confused with criminality because law enforcement has a duty to report and deal with crime. South Sudanese men are deeply hurt, even those who do not show it doesn't mean it isn't there, but that it has been contained so tightly inside for so long that when the lid breaks it comes with collateral damage. There are three common experiences seen among these men: either the man becomes easily angered by those closest to him such as his wife and children, which then turns into family and domestic violence; they become depressed and channel that depression into excessive social media usage and substance abuse; or they wake up one day and decide that they have had enough here in the west where the hierarchy of a family starts with women, followed by children and pets, and leaves men last so they pack their suitcases and go back to South Sudan, leaving wives and children here alone as if they will soon return back. No one of these three types is better than the other because they all result in negative consequences on the man himself, his children, wife, the community and the justice system. There are no role models for the emerging generation of men in the diaspora because the men above them are either dead, too muted by their own trauma to give and set a good example of manhood, or have packed their suitcases and headed back to South Sudan.

The second dimension of the challenges facing South Sudanese young men and boys is their locality and the negative experiences that come with being an outsider such as racism and discrimination. Among these young men there are talents, innovative ideas, creativity, intelligence and dreams but these are suppressed because these young men do not fit into the template of what talented and innovative men should look like or be. These young men are too different for this society, too different in their physical appearance, too different in their accents, and too different in their cultural and racial background. The Caucasian man's society makes sure our young men's ideas and dreams are compressed and given very limited chance to show above the surface. These young men feel hopeless, desperate and see no future in living justly or doing right. These levels of suppression and poverty lead to nothing but destruction and violent outbursts as our young men are caged away like animals behind high brick fences topped with razor wire, and in the worst cases their lives are lost to preventable deaths.

What's missing from all this is that almost all South Sudanese men in the diaspora are not active agents of their lives, they are subjects of a small group of men who have made themselves the decision makers for all men. What's missing is the total absence of what we call a common good among all men that includes the young men. It is no longer enough for these young men to negotiate and navigate their own manhood alone; it needs a collective agreement, a collective responsibility and collective navigation and negotiation by his two parents, by the men in their individual communities and from the minority of men that still feel the need, find it in their hearts and believe in raising young men with good masculine identities. It is a collective work that requires a collective effort from all.

We should have a motivation to build our young people within our individual communities, even if our young people are rejected by the outside world, they can still feel accepted and at home within our homes and within our community. Let society criminalise them but let's guide, safely discipline and protect them - accept them and give them a safe space to feel at home when they are at home. Criminalisation and marginalisation are something that many migrant men struggle with in the west. These struggles are being experienced at greater levels by our young South Sudanese men in the diaspora who are often treated like second or third-class citizens, all judged based on the actions of one individual person, linked to criminality that deserves maximum punishment.

There is a Dinka saying that, "One rotten onion makes the whole bag smell" but this doesn't mean you have to throw the whole bag away, rather you remove the rotten one and place it aside, trying to salvage it if it is salvageable. When one South Sudanese man has committed a crime, we are seeing all South Sudanese men, young or old, called out as Judas and becoming criminalised as a whole; it becomes a South Sudanese race issue rather than an individual case. This type of judgement is frustrating and does not leads to a reduction in the issues affecting families but rather contributes more and more to the many frustrations at large.

Chapter Eleven

Masculine Identities Criminalised by Race

While we have learned much from western literature's focus on patriarchy, hegemony and how masculine identities have been socially constructed and how these themes interact with male crime, these themes have also overshadowed the necessity of sustaining important elements of race, class, culture and economic constructions of masculine self-identity. Although feminist criminology theories have paid close attention to masculine identities in light of patriarchy, criminology and gender inequality, the social structures that define masculinities must also be highlighted to see the full picture.

Despite the various social and environmental factors that might influence men's ideas and beliefs on gender violence and intimate partner violence, it is fair to say that many cultures do not totally condone "toxic masculinity", a practice of masculinity which causes violence. Society is contradicted - with one hand it condemns toxic masculinity while on the other it celebrates the attributes and performance of some groups of men. We must look too, to the structural social conditions that can influence the use of violence as a practice or display of masculine identities. In western society, we understand masculinity as a representation of being able-bodied, preferably Caucasian and middle-class. Class influences masculine identities and therefore when we talk about the masculinity or violent crimes of South Sudanese men, social class and race cannot be ignored. Caucasian men have never seen the need to change their ways to accommodate a greater equality among men of a different race as they have always been superior in their social and economic positions while Black men or nationalities other than White have fewer privileges and opportunities. It is important to take on the social and historical context when we talk about violence among young men as it informs, but does not justify, some of the South Sudanese men's actions.

It is important to understand also that these masculinities include the domination of men as well as women, refugee men such as South Sudanese fit into this category well based on the racial, social and economic structural differences they currently face in the west. The power imbalance between groups of men disadvantages those who sits at the lower end of the power spectrum – a group mostly made up of migrant men and young people of migrant communities such as the South Sudanese.

The high visibility of toxic masculinity in South Sudanese men

The unique and distinctive physical appearance of South Sudanese men in the diaspora has come with many challenges and has contributed to the media's portrayal of Black South Sudanese men. Large group gatherings are labelled as organised "African gangs" and have been referred to as groups of "outlaw thugs" on media outlets. Politicians, too, have used this negative image of South Sudanese-Australian males as part of their tough on crime campaign in an attempt to win a federal government election. In the Australian city of Melbourne, this has caused fear and moral panic among those who are not of African descent about socialising in public where an African group might also be socialising. Negative profiling has contributed to the alienation of South Sudanese men; it seems that differences in physical appearance such as skin colour are a significant issue for many westerners who may have had little contact or interaction with people of different races such as South Sudanese before the wave of immigration in the late 1990s. The image of South Sudanese men has been linked to violence and deviance on many occasions, creating bias in equity and access to social services.

South Sudanese men have formed a part of a visible difference among minority groups settled in the diaspora. When discussing the issues concerning South Sudanese men and violence, we must also take note of age, race, appearance and everyday encounters of racism, as these are fuel to an engine of violent behaviour. Discrimination and racism based on visible differences exist even at the grassroots level in institutions such as primary and secondary schools.[18] The 2016 Australian census showed us that the South Sudanese community has a higher percentage of relatively younger generations compared to the general Australian population.[19] Most crime statistics and discussion around perpetration of criminal activities do not take into account the age demographics of the South Sudanese population in the diaspora, which would help to explain their over-representation in criminal activities in public and private spaces. Since our settlement in western countries, race and physical appearance have been at the forefront for many when it comes to criminal labelling.

When we talk about the South Sudanese and crime, we cannot afford to overlook the fact that race and ethnicity rather than past traumas and settlement challenges do indeed play a role in contemporary law enforcement, education, employment agencies, and within other social institutions and that this affects South Sudanese men; South Sudanese men are hyper-visible in the criminal justice system when compared to other social areas. The problem of over-representation and stereotypes that link South Sudanese men to criminal activities in the diaspora is not an issue of gender inequality alone, but an issue of past traumas, settlement challenges, race, class, gender and a limited knowledge of the diaspora's norms and laws.

Power in the law and the alienation of South Sudanese men

In a recent study on attitudes towards cultural diversity and of the immigrant experience in Australia, it was found that nearly 60 per cent of Indigenous Australians reported experiencing discrimination.[20] These figures are, however, lower than those of African groups which all reported higher rates of discrimination with the South Sudanese rating at nearly 80 per cent.[21] This demonstrates the extreme marginalisation experienced by South Sudanese men and families in their new host country, which in many cases treats them as aliens leading to further suffering, feelings of alienation and increasing struggles by the South Sudanese to accept a lower socioeconomic status. Although some of the offences of South Sudanese men do appear to relate to forms of hegemonic masculinity, they need to be understood in relation to their marginalisation as lower-class, 'Black' refugee men. It is reminiscent of a quote by Karl Marx, "Men make their own history, but they do not make it just as they please; they do not make it under self-selected circumstances, but under circumstances existing already, given and transmitted from the past."[22]

The long traditionally embedded power dynamic in western laws alienates certain groups of men – this is what has been termed structural violence: the social, political, cultural, economic, and historical factors that empower White men and shape the inequality and suffering of others such as the South Sudanese and considers the roles of different types of marginalisation such as racism, social class and poverty in creating lived experiences that are fundamentally less equal. Structural violence helps to explain the multiple and often intersecting forces that create and perpetuate inequality on multiple levels, both for individuals and communities.[23] It is important that we do not view structural violence as separate from the interpersonal family crisis and violence that occurs on the micro level of our individual families but instead comprehend the overlap in structural violence shaping micro forms of violence, which places groups such as South Sudanese in vulnerable positions.

There is a relationship between structural violence and family crisis that often stems from men's inequality, as the vast majority of middle-class White men run powerful organisations that influence societies and inform individuals' decisions. It is difficult for newly arrived South Sudanese men to fully engage in discussions of social equity between men and women when they experience social marginalisation and discrimination from other groups of men. South Sudanese men's participation in employment, education and other social inclusion activities to enhance different forms of capital and minimise feelings of alienation and social exclusion should be the focus and starting point for discussions on social equality.

Racism lives on, sometimes overtly but most times subconsciously, no matter what government policies and regulations there are around discrimination. Recent research following the Melbourne Moomba riots in 2016, reported clear evidence that the South Sudanese are experiencing a high level of racism in Victoria, Australia.[24] This evidence and the experiences of racism and discrimination have significantly impacted and influenced the experiences of the South Sudanese living in Victoria.

Chapter Twelve

It is not Easy being South Sudanese Men in the Diaspora

In a real sense all life is interrelated. All men are caught in an inescapable network of mutuality, tied in a single garment of destiny. Whatever affects one directly, affects all indirectly. I can never be what I ought to be until you are what you ought to be, and your related structure of reality.

Martin Luther King Jr.

Male or female, we can agree that our lives are interconnected and interchangeable. What affects South Sudanese men directly affects South Sudanese women and children indirectly. Our social issues are intersectional and interconnected, however, this realisation has not been reflected as much as it should be in the existing literature and discussion on acts of violence and in areas of many other life challenges. There is a lot of correction that needs to be done: correction through the systems, correction by parents through self-reflection and evaluation, correction by the young people, correction by families and by the wider society. The systems such as the justice system in the diaspora need to make room for minority groups of men such as South Sudanese men to have an active involvement in positive programs that address their own individual needs. For instance, a lack of male-specific services or positive programs that address core issues other than negative behaviour for South Sudanese men are minimal and this permits very little room for positive change. We should not wait until a crime is committed then mandate them into programs such as the Men's Behaviour Change Program which is very western in theory and delivery.

In order to contribute to and develop the discussion on South Sudanese masculinities and their relations with acts of violence, our ultimate goal should aim to firstly normalise South Sudanese men-led conversations and to create impactful knowledge that acknowledges our men's past traumatic experiences, current social inequalities and language barriers, rather than reproducing and enforcing western standards of gender identities. For instance, when service providers identify a man's lack of engagement in seeking help, it is just as important to examine the current service model's limitations in enabling that man to seek help, rather than only acknowledging the level of disengagement which then often escalates to crisis levels where they are forced by dire circumstances to seek help. One way to decolonise these complexities is by allowing these marginalised South Sudanese men to have a voice, to be at the centre of their own lived experiences, to speak on issues they are facing that contribute to experiences of micro and macro violence, and bring a reality of our men as active agents in equality, peaceful and respectful relationships within their immediate families and in their current society.

Crimes such as family and domestic violence are an interrelated reality that directly affect women and men and indirectly affect children. There is no one single preventative approach of gender violence that excludes men in general, and further excludes marginalised men from the process of its deeper understanding and potential solutions that could lead to its ending without the inclusion of both genders in this critical discussion. Women and children can never be free from experiences of family violence if we are exclusive about which men and which groups of male voices and experiences are presented and represented in our discussions on the subject.

The conversation that is needed should be about understanding what has been and is happening to women but also what is happening with men and with the whole family. The family and domestic violence view that men do it for power and control does not acknowledge other intersectional areas of suffering that men of migrant and refugee communities in the diaspora are experiencing, and has even less to say about driving factors such as men's vulnerabilities and the traumatic experiences that contribute to perpetrations of domestic violence. A common theme in academic and non-academic papers on the subject of South Sudanese men's violence towards women is the changes to gender roles, which see women becoming more involved in providing for the family and acquiring their own financial support, and the challenge for men to accept this drastic shift in traditionally understood roles. It is interesting, however, that this argument often lacks the inclusion of men's perspectives as to why they might be finding this change challenging, most simply state that they do. In most cases, the challenges that South Sudanese men face due to shifting gender roles is not due to the changes in roles in itself but the misconceptions, the condescension, the mannerism, the disrespect and manipulative attitudes that comes with it from some women after they have acquired a kind of "empowerment".

Many men in the South Sudanese community have no issue with their wife being a breadwinner or co-provider. In fact, it gives them a sense of security and lifts the burden of living on a single income off their shoulders. Many South Sudanese families have relatives back home or in camps who they support on top of their living expenses in the diaspora, so the more income the family have, the better the financial situation is for everyone in the immediate and extended family. You can see why men wouldn't resist their wife getting a job and pulling her economic weight. The only reason for men to be reluctant for the wife to get a job is if she has a health problem preventing her to work or when they have many children that are very young and need to be fully attended, say, when most of the children are in primary school. South Sudanese families are often large and most of them have many children born one after another. For instance, a family can have a child in every year level at primary school as well as older children in high school. From this aspect, it is common sense to want the wife to be a stay home mum if the husband works full-time.

Researching and writing about these kinds of complexities, vulnerabilities, and uncertainties of South Sudanese men has the potential to empower them by starting the inclusion of marginalised men's voices into critical discussions, and supporting this group of men to negotiate their masculinities in complex ways. There's a need for agency and reflexivity and for South Sudanese men's actions in family violence to be prioritised in research on masculinities. The process of allowing marginalised men such as South Sudanese men in the west to share their experiences, aspirations; pain and trauma acquired during the war, in refugee camps and how that has affected what it means to be a "man" on the one hand, with the practical realities and their daily struggles in their current society on the other, may be beneficial in understanding their contribution to victimisations, interventions and perpetrations of family violence which bring upon family crisis.

It might be safe to presume that this process would permit service providers, policy makers and the criminal justice system to recognise the precariousness of these men's own masculine vulnerabilities and, in particular, how destructive the devotion to singular gender stereotypes could be to South Sudanese men, as well as to women in the South Sudanese community. This approach is an innovative effort to broadly engage men in the South Sudanese community in interventions and preventions with a strong focus on developing and promoting liberated masculinities rather than marginalised masculinities that result in frustration and anger.

As revealed in this book, the most esteemed attributes of manhood for South Sudanese men consist of heterosexual marriage, economic breadwinning, physical and emotional strength, fatherhood and independence. These are embodied practices of manhood, deeply infused with power and linked to one another. In the diaspora, South Sudanese men's financial and social powers may enable him to function as a heteronormative breadwinner which, in the South Sudanese cultures, affords a higher chance of being respected by those immediate to him such as his intimate partner and children and the community more broadly. While this could be interpreted as hegemonic in nature, it does not necessarily hurt women in the South Sudanese traditional culture or in other forms of masculinities. For many gender critical writers, the idea of gender hegemony is a complex construct and hence multiple hegemonies could articulate the social context for South Sudanese men.

Living in poverty, mentally embedded experiences of trauma from war and refugee camps, social inequalities and poor mental health in South Sudanese men can be incredibly frustrating and disempowering, and is exacerbated by a limited number of viable opportunities to strengthen their masculinities and construct alternative masculinities without resorting to violence. While South Sudanese in the diaspora are deeply invested and committed to their cultural obligations of being protectors and providers for their families, it appears most of them are suffering within a system which is failing them. This system frustrates South Sudanese men, yet the criminal justice system and the current society requires them to maintain respectful relationships, achieve social power and positioning in the gender hierarchies by adequately fulfilling varying ideals of masculinity. Acknowledging the range of conflicting forces, ambiguities, and vulnerabilities among

South Sudanese men in the diaspora is an important contribution to scholarship on violence and family breakdown that gives a simplistic representation of the meaning of manhood.

Arrests, punishments and the criminalisation of many South Sudanese men, young and old, for minor crimes are only a form of hygiene for what has been labelled as toxic masculinity, not a cure. Hygiene can contain the spread of the disease, in this case the violent outbursts but it does not cure the cause. The cure is and shall be found in going through a diagnostic process, going back to study and understand their background and root causes so that such undesirable criminal behaviours can be addressed, maybe cured or even to be punished accordingly if need be. I will conclude by using the words from the American Declaration of Independence as I think that these words are important for many nations and all mankind and should be the experience of all, "All men are created equal, that they are endowed by their Creator with certain unalienable Rights, that among these are Life, Liberty and the Pursuit of Happiness." Unfortunately, these are not the realities of all or many men, they are realities that belong only to small group of men who are privileged, hold positions of power within the social constructs of mankind and have the greater means and resources than the other. In this day and age, it is not easy to be a man but it's even more difficult to be a South Sudanese migrant man on foreign land, in the diaspora.

CHAPTER THIRTEEN

An Open Letter to South Sudanese Men

Dear South Sudanese men in the diaspora,

You all thought you could swim in the deep seas of your struggles in these foreign lands, until you started to drown. We know that in being a South Sudanese man, one of the many masculine attributes you possess is being tough and strong even under circumstances where you need to show your emotions. This is no longer serving you; it's no longer serving your family or serving our community. There is nothing wrong with being sad, being disappointed, being frustrated or even being angry. It is the manner in which you release these emotions that can either harm or improve your life and the livelihood of those around you such as your family and community.

Here in the diaspora, your new society are struggling to understand you, they are struggling to make sense of who you are and your emotions as men of a different culture and ethnic background. They might not notice your tears, they might not notice your sadness, and they might not notice your pain but they sure do notice your mistakes – mistakes that happen when you burst out in anger, mistakes that happen when you leave your children and wife to move overseas because the west has made no place for you, and mistakes that stop you from searching for ways to improve your lives because of all the obstacles and barriers that are in the way. Agonise over these many challenges you have had and are now facing but be organised in the way in which your agony manifests. Let's put an end to violence and dysfunction in our families by looking within.

My uncles and my brothers, I do understand that the hostility of the war and camp conditions did not stop from the moment you ceased fire or left the camps; that the trauma and pain live on beyond the final days of fighting, of running for refuge and settlement but I still urge you to go and agonise over all that you have been through, but be organised. Let us organise ourselves for the sake of our future, for the sake of our young people's future and most importantly for the sake of all our ancestors who have endured a long and endless suffering that only death did them part. If they were to see your current ways of functioning as South Sudanese men, many of them would be deeply hurt and ashamed and would wonder what happened to the true South Sudanese manhood; they would wonder what happened to the integrity, the humility, the courage, the respect for yourselves, respect for your women, respect for your loved ones, for your lineage, for your community and for your society as a whole. What happened to our gerontocratic ways of keeping peace in our homes; what happened to shame and the willingness to teach your young people to be good men, to carry on the good name of their family? What you do as fathers, older brothers and husbands shows greatly in our young people. Our young people are currently flooding the criminal justice system, partly because they are not seeing good role models in our homes. You have starved them of the role of a good father, and when they see you maltreat their mother, they think that is the way to treat a woman and so their own relationships don't work out simply because they don't know any better. The cycle continues.

Young men are going around with anger. When they are out of your sight, they are more likely to project that same anger onto their peers or somebody else. You, as fathers, although our history and currently environment has morally paralysed many you, we still look up to you to transfer the wisdom, the education and guidelines of life onto this current younger generation. You need to acknowledge your part in the dysfunction that is going on within our families and particularly among our young men. You, as fathers, need to ask yourselves, 'What is my contribution to this dynamic that I have to change, to improve or to work in the best interest of my family, of my community and of our society?' Because young people learn by seeing just as much as by doing, and when they see you are not interested, that you are maltreating the mother or other men, they internalise that hurt that comes from seeing you behave or act a certain way. Although many of you intend to be good fathers and husbands, most times you don't translate those good intentions into habits, decisions and practicality so you end up starving the family, especially the boy-child and the mother off a good father and a husband. We all need each other in order to make and keep healthy and happy families. Women are the fountain of life and when they are affected the whole household is affected, so how you treat them matters.

We all need each other if we are going to survive life in the west. A husband needs a good wife, a wife needs a good husband and most importantly children need good, active, emotionally, physically and mentally present parents. Not one, but both parents! For single parent homes led by a single mother or father, you need a positive male role models for the children, especially the boys. If we don't open our minds to ways that we can change our current situation and different ways of doing in the diaspora, we'll soon add to the world's growing numbers of what experts call "broken homes, dysfunctional families and vulnerable families". This kind of labelling is often used here in the west not only to describe certain families but help broadcast the family's failures by bringing them to the public arena, which also affects kids and young people in school and in other areas of social and economic gatherings. For young people there will be that internal stigma and internal belief that one might not have a better future because of their past, which, once the family has been given this label, leads to a lack of interest to improve or to try harder in accomplishing personal goals and ambitions. We currently have increasing numbers of our young men in the criminal justice system and we need to ask ourselves, "What is the future of those who are still at home as well as those in the criminal justice system?" Those in the system due to minor crimes will eventually be released, and without proper systems and support from their families and community post-release, some of them are at risk of becoming homeless, drug addicts and with mental health issues. This is not so far away when we think of the future that we should foresee. Some of these issues are facing us now and might not improve but worsen with time if nothing is done about it.

They say that "The future belongs to those who prepare for it." What are we preparing; how are you, how are we preparing for such a future? Instead of ignoring it or leaving the responsibility entirely to the service providers and the criminal justice system, we need to take responsibility and actions that will make what Dr John Garang De Mabior has called the "seeds" of South Sudan grow. You came to the diaspora as seeds that would better their own lives, their family's lives and the lives of those around them and the ones left behind, but looking at our ways of functionalities currently in the diaspora, those seeds are rapidly getting spoiled.

Our young boys of whom some are your sons, brothers and friends are dropping dead every now and then. If they're not stabbing each other, they're going to juvenile detention, and if they're not going to juvenile we are losing them to suicide. All heart breaking options. For instance, in Australia in 2019, the community lost many young people to suicide. The following year of 2020, Kot's family of Melbourne, Victoria lost two sons, Machar Kot and Kon Kot (may their souls rest in peace), both to knife-crime within a six-month period. Machar was stabbed and died in June and just before Christmas, on the 22nd of December, Kon was also killed in the same manner. Both young men were under the age of 25 and their offenders were also young people. If the fact that one family can lose two sons not to natural death but to knife-crime within a period of six months does not alarm the community, the parents and the fathers, then I really don't know what will. We need to ask ourselves individually and collectively, why our young men no longer want to live, why they are so angry and what can be done to prevent these premature deaths and imprisonments. This takes me back to my previous point of fathers' provision and the presence of a father in a young boy and man's life. Provision does not always have to translate to physical things such as money because we know that most men are not financially where they would like to be and have had limited opportunities to change that, but just being present is sometime enough for these young people. I understand not all men have the capacity to provide, but being there, teaching, inspiring and setting certain values and morals into the boy-child is a huge part of provision that many fathers are failing these young men by not being able to fill these gaps. Having said that, many families are still alive and well today because of your bravery to protect them during the war and you should never forget that. My biggest wish and I would assume that it is the wish of many young South Sudanese persons in the diaspora, is to live in a loving and peaceful home, with loving parents in a united violence-free family. You can be those loving parents and you can be the ones making those loving and peaceful violence-free homes! However, this can only take place once you as an individual start looking within, have a self-surgery of examining your deep wounds and start healing the wounds so you can stop bleeding on those around you. Indulging in substances, wasting time on social media making vulgar live videos, attacking one another and behaving violently either verbally, emotionally, or physically does nothing but leads to self-distraction and detrimental repercussions on your family and those around you.

My heartiest wish for you all is to find peace, inclusion, healing and justice.

Yours sincerely,

Akuch Kuol Anyieth

Endnotes and Resources

1 Johnson, D. (2016). Front Matter. In *The Root Causes of Sudan's Civil Wars: Old Wars and New Wars (Expanded 3rd Edition)* (pp. I-Iv). Woodbridge, Suffolk; Rochester, NY: Boydell & Brewer. doi:10.7722/j.ctt1h64pck.1

2 Litz, B. T., Stein, N., Delaney, E., Lebowitz, L., Nash, W. P., Silva, C., & Maguen, S. (2009). Moral injury and moral repair in war Veterans: A preliminary model and intervention strategy. *Clinical Psychology Review, 29*(8), 695-706. http://doi.org/10.1016/j.cpr.2009.07.003 Shay, J. (2014). Moral injury. *Psychoanalytic Psychology, 31*(2), 182-191. https://doi.org/10.1037/a0036090

3 Griffin, B. J., Purcell, N., Burkman, K., Litz, B. T., Bryan, C. J., Schmitz, M., Villierme, C., Walsh, J., & Maguen, S. (2019). Moral injury: An integrative review. *Journal of Traumatic Stress, 32*(3), 350-362. https://doi.org/10.1002/jts.22362

4 Farnsworth, J. K., Drescher, K. D., Nieuwsma, J. A., Walser, R. B., & Currier, J. M. (2014). The role of moral emotions in military trauma: Implications for the study and treatment of moral injury. *Review of General Psychology, 18*(4), 249-262, https://doi.org/10.1037/gpr0000018

5 Australian Human Rights Commission. (2010). *In Our Own Words: African Australian*; A review of human rights and social inclusion issues

6 Abur, William. (2018). Systemic vilification and racism are affecting on the South Sudanese community in Australia.

7 Gottfredson, M. R., & Hirschi, T. (1990). *A general theory of crime.* Stanford University Press. Quinney, R. (1977). Class, state, and crime: On the theory and practice of criminal justice.

8 Front Matter. (2012). In Moynagh M. & Forestell N. (Eds.), *Documenting First Wave Feminisms: Volume 1: Transnational Collaborations and Crosscurrents* (pp. I-Vi). Toronto; Buffalo; London: University ofToronto Press. Retrieved January 5, 2021, from http://www.jstor.org/stable/10.3138/9781442664098.

9 Evans, J. (1998). *Feminist theory today: An introduction to second-wave feminism.* SAGE Publications Ltd, https://www.doi.org/10.4135/9781446222140

10 Drake, J. (1997). Third Wave Feminisms. *Feminist Studies, 23*(1), 97-108. doi:10.2307/3178299

11 Front Matter. (2003). In Lewis R. & Mills S. (Eds.), *Feminist Postcolonial Theory: A Reader* (pp. I-Iv). Edinburgh: Edinburgh University Press. doi:10.3366/j.ctvxcr9q0.1

12 Anzaldúa, G. and C. Moraga, (eds.) (1981). This Bridge Called My Back: Writings by Radical Women of Color. New York, Kitchen Table Press. Boyce Davies, C and A. Graves, (eds.) (1986). Ngambika: Studies ofWomen in African Literature. Trenton, NJ, Africa World Press.

13 Alexander Pope (Written 1709, published 1711). In *An Essay on Criticism* 14.

14 Götz Egloff and Dragana Djordjevic (April 17th 2019). Challenges for Behavioral Neuroscience: Prenatal, Postnatal, and Social Factors, Behavioral Neuroscience, Sara Palermo and Rosalba Morese, IntechOpen, DOI: 10.5772/intechopen.85368. Available from: https://www.intechopen.com/books/behavioral-neuroscience/challenges-for-behavioral-neuroscience-prenatal-postnatal-and-social-factors

15 Kofman O. (2002). The role of prenatal stress in the etiology of developmental behavioural disorders. *Neuroscience and biobehavioral reviews*, *26*(4), 457–470. https://doi.org/10.1016/s0149-7634(02)00015-5

16 Austin, Phil & Priest, S. (2005). Clinical issues in perinatal mental health: New developments in the detection and treatment of perinatal mood and anxiety disorders. Acta psychiatrica Scandinavica. 112. 97-104. 10.1111/j.1600-0447.2005.00549.x.

17 Hines, M., Spencer, D., Kung, K. T., Browne, W. V., Constantinescu, M., & Noorderhaven, R. M. (2016). The early postnatal period, mini-puberty, provides a window on the role of testosterone in human neurobehavioural development. *Current opinion in neurobiology*, *38*, 69–73. https://doi.org/10.1016/j.conb.2016.02.008

18 Baak, Melanie. (2018). Racism and Othering for South Sudanese heritage students in Australian schools: is inclusion possible?. International Journal of Inclusive Education. 23. 1-17. 10.1080/13603116.2018.1426052.

19 Australian Bureau of Statistics. 2016. Australian Census

20 Kamp, A., Alam, O., Blair, K. and Dunn, K. 2017. Australians' Views on Cultural Diversity, Nation and Migration, 2015-16. Cosmopolitan Civil Societies: an Interdisciplinary Journal. 9(3), 61-84. http://dx.doi.org/10.5130/ccs.v9i 3.5635

21 Kamp, A., Alam, O., Blair, K. and Dunn, K. 2017. Australians' Views on Cultural Diversity, Nation and Migration, 2015-16. Cosmopolitan Civil Societies: an Interdisciplinary Journal. 9(3), 61-84. http://dx.doi.org/10.5130/ccs.v9i 3.5635

22 Marx, Karl, 1818-1883. (1951). The eighteenth Brumaire of Louis Bonaparte. Translated by Daniel De Leon. New York, New York: Labor News.

23 Farmer, P. (1996). On Suffering and Structural Violence: A View from Below. *Daedalus, 125*(1), 261-283. Retrieved January 6, 2021, from http://www.jstor.org/stable/20027362

24 Benier, Kathryn & Blaustein, Jarrett & Johns, Diana & Maher, Sara. (2018). 'Don't drag me into this': Growing up South Sudanese in Victoria after the 2016 Moomba 'riot'. 10.13140/RG.2.2.21330.40643.

Documentaries and videos

The late SPLA leader Dr. John Garang speech of encouragement to boys' soldiers in 1989

Dr. John Garang speaking to Jech Amer - Jebel Raat. (1989). https://youtu.be/D0jXiUIAcIg Accessed 10th January 2021

Sudan People's Liberation Army. (SPLA). https://www.youtube.com/watch?v=K9odM1BFHQk Accessed 10th January 2021

This is a documentary about armed conflict in the Bahr El Ghazal region in southern Sudan.

The Secret Story: Looking at the Roots of Conflict in South Sudan's Bahr El Ghazal Region. (1998). https://www.youtube.com/watch?v=shQaJ5qDSjM Accessed 10th January 2021

Nine News. (2020). Two brothers died to knives crimes in Melbourne Victoria within six months. Accessed https://www.9news.com.au/national/man-dies-after-fight-in-caroline-springs-melbourne/8c8ffeb1-73e8-4db7-ae72-90a94bbcfef8 12th January 2021

Acknowledgements

According to a famous African proverb, "It takes a village to raise a child". I feel as though I was a child and would have never been able to complete this book without the tremendous support of the village "the South Sudanese community".

To Peter Lual Deng from Africa World Books Publishing, your encouragement and support have aided the birth of this book. Your guidance has enabled me to remain calm and achieve more than I thought possible in such a short amount of time.

To my friend and also editor, Elizabeth Carr, I would like to thank you for your constructive feedback, advice and support.

To my parents, my siblings, my nieces and nephews, your continued support throughout my life have helped me keep my sanity. Your unwavering emotional and spiritual supports have given me the strength I could never have found anywhere else. You all have always stood firm in support of my education. You are all my rock; I love you and I hope I make you feel proud and appreciated.

To my friends, Akuol Manyok and Grace Michira, thank you all very much; you have been there through moments of emotional breakdown. I am blessed to have friends like you two.

www.ingramcontent.com/pod-product-compliance
Lightning Source LLC
Chambersburg PA
CBHW021205110726
47900CB00002B/735